ack, N.Y. Res. of P.G. TEN EYCK.

The Troy Savings Bank
is privileged to make available
this limited edition of
A Resourceful People:
A Pictorial History of Rensselaer County
This is the story of
the men and women and their families
who worked and inspired a community
to build cultural, commercial, educational,
industrial, and charitable enterprises
of which we are justly proud.

We dedicate this book
to the residents
of Rensselaer County—
past, present and future.

The Troy Savings Bank

A Resourceful People

A Pictorial History of Rensselaer County, New York

by

Rachel D. Bliven
Robert N. Andersen
G. Steven Draper
Eva Gemmill
Hughes Gemmill
Joseph A. Parker
Helen M. Upton

for

The Rensselaer County Historical Society

This Berlin farmscape was photographed by
J. F. Cowee. *Courtesy of Rensselaer County
Historical Society*

The Donning Company/Publishers
5659 Virginia Beach Boulevard
Norfolk, Virginia 23502

Edited by Valerie von Weich

Library of Congress Cataloging-in-Publication Data

A Resourceful people.

Bibliography: p.
Includes index.
1. Rensselaer County (N.Y.)—History—Pictorial works.
2. Rensselaer County (N.Y.)—Description and travel—Views.
I. Bliven, Rachel D. II. Rensselaer County
Historical Society.
F127.R3R46   1987   974.7'41   87-27264
ISBN 0-89865-610-9

Printed in the United States of America

Contents

Foreword

For many years the Rensselaer County Historical Society has recognized the need for an updated history of the county which it serves. The last general history of Troy and Rensselaer County was written by Rutherford Hayner and published by the Lewis Historical Publishing Company in 1925. Taking up where Hayner left off, Joseph A. Parker published *Looking Back: A History of Troy and Rensselaer County 1925-1980* in 1982, capturing many of the changes of the last six decades. The present publication attempts to bring together under one cover all of the county's history up to 1987, answering an almost critical need for information on our local history sparked, in part, by the celebration of the nation's Bicentennial and by a new interest in industrial history and historic preservation. Local history is that swarm of names, dates, occurrences, and developments which took place in any small corner of our nation. It is both a reflection of national trends and an integral part of them. Once the step-child of academic historians, local history is now receiving unprecedented scrutiny by scholars, students, and the public in almost equal measure. Books are written, films and audio-visual programs produced, cities revitalized, and school curricula developed based on local history.

Such attention demands current information, and, in the best of all possible worlds, information based on current historiographical thought. For small historical agencies this is a formidable task and one infrequently achieved. However, a start can be made, and the publication of *A Resourceful People* is an exciting opportunity to bring to the public a history of Rensselaer County which records information of the 1980s as well as the 1780s and in a small way covers issues of current historical concern, such as immigration, leisure time, educational trends and governmental reorganization.

Finding a single author for such a publication proved difficult. Because many fine local historians with expert knowledge of their areas exist in Rensselaer County, the Society chose to work with a team of authors. Each author was assigned to deal with a general subject area in which he or she was already somewhat of an authority, and then to flesh out this general background with local facts. The Society further assigned a captain to the team to coordinate the material and provide a homogeneity to the publication.

None of this, of course, would have been possible without the gracious sponsorship of the Troy Savings Bank and the professional expertise of the Donning Company/Publishers. Both organizations cooperated with the Society and its team to produce a publication in a very limited time.

Thus *A Resourceful People* is itself the result of the teamwork of a dedicated and resourceful group whose herculean efforts are hereby gratefully acknowledged by the Society, and, we trust, will be appreciated by all the people of Rensselaer County and those interested in its history.

Breffny A. Walsh, *Director*
Rensselaer County Historical Society

Acknowledgments

Silas Jones, a Revolutionary War veteran, left his New England home after the war and moved to the Petersburg area to farm, an occupation his ten sons eventually took up as well. Here are some of his descendants gathered in Petersburg for a family reunion about 1930. *Courtesy of Judy Rowe*

W e gratefully acknowledge the following individuals, organizations, and institutions, who have given of their time, shared information and photographs, and assisted us in numerous small ways: Albany International, Felt Division, Bertil Engh, comptroller; Thomas Aulita, P. E., Clifton Knolls; Gene Avery, Hoosick Falls; Malcolm Bell, chemist, East Greenbush; Berlin Historical Society, Katherine Wells; Nancy Bernstein, Petersburg; Wayne Brown, Rensselaer; Brunswick Historical Society, Mildred McChesney; Capital District Transportation Authority; Sanford Catlin, Poestenkill; Walter Catricala, Troy; Ethel Center, Rensselaer; City of Rensselaer Planning Department; Cluett Peabody Company, James Morske, Richard Purcell, Troy; Detroit Institute of Art; Diocese of Albany, Margaret Sickles, public relations; Duffers Scientific, Dr. Hugo Ferguson, Poestenkill; Emma Willard School, Kenneth Brock, archivist; John E. Finegan, Troy; Flomatic, Joan Nealon, Hoosick Falls; Mrs. Harold Fox, West Sand Lake; Josephine Fraser, Rensselaer; Fritz Helmbold Inc., Marilyn Ogden, Troy; James P. Griffith, Schenectady; Mrs. Rynard Gundrum, Grafton; Mrs. Charles Gutermuth, Berlin; Henry J. Seagroatt Company, James Riccardi, Berlin; Milton Hill, Poestenkill; The Historical Society of Esquatak, Lynn Richards, president, Lauretta Harris, archivist, Castleton-on-Hudson; Hoosac School, Anne Bugbee, vice-principal, Hoosick; Hoosick Falls Historical Society, Harold Robson; Hoosick Historical Society, George Peer; Hudson-Mohawk Industrial Gateway, Terry L. Winslow, executive director; Hudson Valley Community College, Kenneth Williams, archivist; Frank Hull, Poestenkill; LeRoy Johnson, Sr., Troy; Herman and Mary Kosegarten, Nassau; Irene Schumann Kropp, Poestenkill; Alice Lawrence, Rensselaer; Dean H. Leith, Jr., Brunswick; Richard Lohnes, Schaghticoke; Philip Lord, Hoags Corners; Thelma Mahoney, Grafton; Keith Marvin, Menands; Mercer Companies, Inc., Albany; Miller Museum, Edith Beaumont, curator, Hoosick Falls; Nelson's Used Book Store, Troy; New

9

York State Office of Parks, Recreation and Historic Preservation, Bureau of Historic Sites, Paul R. Huey, senior scientist (archaeology), Waterford; Norplex-Oak, James Shaw, Hoosick Falls; John Peckham, Brunswick; David Phillips, North Greenbush; Sue Putnam, town clerk, Grafton; Frank Raymond, Grafton; The Record Newspapers, Roland Blais, editor, Sue Ness, librarian, Troy; Frederick Reichard, Poestenkill; Rensselaer County Council for the Arts, Troy; Rensselaer County Junior Museum, Ralph Pascale, Troy; Rensselaer County Planning Department, Jamie Lahut, Troy; Rensselaer County Sewer District No. 1, Fred J. Wurtemberger; Rensselaer Polytechnic Institute, John Dojka, Institute archivist/head of special collections, Robert Whitaker, Troy; Rensselaer Public Library, Kenneth Ryder; Rensselaer Technology Park, Ann Kerwin; William Reynolds, historian, Berlin; Judy Rowe, researcher/lecturer, Glass Lake; Leonard S. Schell, East Greenbush; Helen Stover Sharpe, Albany; Jim Shaughnessy, Troy; Standard Manufacturing Co., Inc., George Arakelian, Troy; Sterling Drug Inc., Margery Laird, New York City; Mrs. Dean P. Taylor, Troy; Lawrence Torpey, Hoosick Falls; *Trains* magazine, George Drury, librarian; Troy Planning Department, Ruth Pierpont, David Saehrig; Troy Public Library; Valley Falls Library, Freda Stark, librarian; Mrs. Charles Vannier, West Sand Lake; Veteran Scout Association, Leonard Filsen, chairman of board, Albany; Charles H. Viens, West Sand Lake; Visilox Systems, Inc., George DuJack, Poestenkill; Mrs. Robert Wagner, Poestenkill; Newton Wiley, Pittstown; Edmund J. Winslow, senior historian, State of New York.

We are fortunate in New York to have officially designated historians for every town. The historians from the many towns and villages of Rensselaer County were invaluable in providing us with detailed local information and photographs. We would especially like to thank: Margaret Kinn, Berlin; Dorothy McChesney, Brunswick; Alice Walsh, Castleton-on-Hudson; Jeanette Barber, East Greenbush; Irma Wagar, Grafton; Joseph Holloway, Hoosick; Jeanette Collamer, Nassau; Karen Hartgen Fisher, North Greenbush; Ellen L. Wiley, Pittstown; Florence Hill, Poestenkill; Madolyn V. Carpenter, Sand Lake; Christina Kelly, Schaghticoke; and Anna B. Bayba, Stephentown.

Frances D. Broderick, Warren F. Broderick, and Shirley Dunn were kind enough to review our manuscript, graciously performing expert services in a short time in checking dates, facts, and omissions.

A pictorial history relies heavily on quality photographs. Primary copywork and much darkroom time was provided by G. Steven Draper and George Mead.

Everyone on the staff of the Rensselaer County Historical Society has contributed in no small way to the publication. The book would truly not have been possible without the patient guidance and unwavering support of Breffny Walsh, executive director. Especially notable were the sometimes lonely efforts of Darlene Suto to keep the ship on course. Beverly Culver and Society volunteer Fulvia Russo offered their services at the copy machine and the telephone. Society volunteer Helen Gardner cheerfully produced library material on demand, and Curator Stacy Pomeroy Draper tracked down crucial items from the collection. The one truly indispensible staff member was Education Director Peggy Ann LaPoint, who sat endless hours at the computer, translating handwriting, organizing and editing the drafts as she entered the text.

Sadly we must recognize posthumously the contribution of K. Jack Bauer, Society trustee. As a nationally recognized widely published historian, his analysis of the project and good practical advice gave us the courage to proceed with the publication.

Last and decidedly not least, we shall always be grateful to our families and friends for helping us to get through this process with health and humor intact.

Preface

The compilation of a pictorial history of Rensselaer County has been an exciting and challenging task, since people have been making this area their home for over three hundred years. Throughout the project, we have sought to find images to make those three hundred years of the past a present reality for our readers. The results, we feel, create a visual scrapbook of our county's history. Each image tells a story which certainly could be elaborated on, yet the pieces form a coherent whole, the visual patchwork of our county's past.

In compiling the images, we have been struck by the amount of material which we have not had room to include. The history of this county is so rich and the pictorial resources so extensive at times that our publication represents only the very tip of the stack. Almost all of the towns and many of the villages have recently published or are in the process of compiling pictures and histories of their areas. We strongly recommend that anyone interested in learning more about the specific towns of Rensselaer County consult the many resources listed in our bibliography.

In compiling the final manuscript many good pictures had to be left out, and gaps inevitably occur. For this, we sincerely apologize and hope that future historians will correct our errors. When forced with difficult choices, we have tried to err on the side of including images of the county, since the city of Troy in particular has been extensively covered in previous publications such as Thomas Phelan's book *The Hudson-Mohawk Gateway: An Illustrated History* and Joseph Parker's *Looking Back: A History of Troy and Rensselaer County 1925-1980.*

The people of our past had faces and walked many of the same streets that we know so well today. Perhaps now we can begin to reintroduce ourselves to them. We offer this collection of images in the hope that it will inspire others to uncover more pictures and to continue to document the vibrant history of this county.

The Authors

The Witenagemot Oak in Schaghticoke was a symbol of peace for the Indians. *Courtesy of Rensselaer County Historical Society*

Chapter One

1607-1790
The Early Years

The 665 square miles of Rensselaer County encompass some of the most varied countryside in the state of New York. Located 150 miles north of New York City and stretching 30 miles along the banks of the Hudson River, the county extends about 20 miles to New York's eastern border, touching Vermont and Massachusetts. Flat alluvial plains along the shore of the river break into rolling hills as they move eastward, rising to the Rensselaer Plateau down the center of the county, dipping into the Hoosic River Valley, and then rising again to the Taconic mountain range. The central plateau, covered with forests, was largely avoided by farmers due to its poor soil. The Ice Age origins of the landscape are quickly seen in the boulder-covered ridges, rounded hills and glacial eskers, as well as the lovely lakes dotting the valley. Scientists have estimated that a mass of ice covered this area for centuries and was as thick as two thousand feet at the site of the city of Troy. Sandstone and conglomerate can be found throughout the county, indicating that this area was also at the edge of a prehistoric seashore some hundreds of millions of years ago, in the days when Lake Albany filled the basin between Poughkeepsie and the Adirondacks, from the Taconics to the Helderbergs. Swift-flowing streams from the high central plateau tumble through the county in deep ravines leading to the Hudson River. Many of these streams—the Wynantskill, Poestenkill, Muitzekill, Valatiekill, Tsatsawassa, and Kinderhook—would provide power for the first industries in Rensselaer County.

Indians were the first inhabitants of this land. Roaming the forests as early as 2000 B.C., they were nomadic hunter-gatherers. Later Indians seemed to have settled in increasingly larger villages by A.D. 1000, growing maize, beans, and squash in fertile river bottom lands. The Mahican Indians' chief village was near what is now Castleton-on-Hudson, and Lansingburgh natives still speak of an Indian castle at 101st Street. Traces of Mahican settlements have also been found in Schaghticoke, Troy, Rensselaer, Nassau Village, Schodack Landing, Hoosick Falls, Sand Lake, and other areas of the county.

In 1609, Henry Hudson, sailing for the Dutch East India Company in search of a sea passage westward to the Indies, discovered the river now named for him and sailed up as far as his ship would go. He came ashore in several places and recorded his impressions of the land and natives in his diary. "It is as pleasant a land as one can tread upon. . .I sailed to the shore in one of their canoes, with an old man, who was the chief of a tribe, consisting of forty men and seventeen women; these I saw there in a house well constructed of oak bark, and circular in shape, with the appearance of having a vaulted ceiling. . . . The land is the finest for cultivation that I ever in my life set foot upon, and it also abounds in trees of every description. The natives are a very good people. . ." (Jameson, *Narratives*). Hudson continued as far north as the current site of Troy, where he determined that the waters were too shallow to continue farther and so turned back to the ocean.

The next few years found fur traders visiting the area to trade with the Indians. By 1624, the Dutch had established Fort Orange on the west bank of the river, at what is now Albany. In 1629 the Dutch West India Company adopted a new plan to settle the area. Tracts of land twenty-four miles long on one bank of the river or twelve miles along both banks were offered to anyone who would, at his own expense, settle fifty people there within four years. The landowner, known as a patroon, would be overlord of the land and his heirs would inherit his privileges. The settlers were to be tenant farmers, owing an annual rent to the patroon.

In 1630-31 Kiliaen Van Rensselaer purchased extensive lands on the west side of the Hudson River extending from modern-day Coeymans north to the Mohawk River and "in width two days' journey inland." A further purchase extended his tract on the east side of the river from a single parcel in today's city of Rensselaer south as far as Castleton. Ultimately the Van Rensselaer family was to own more than 700,000 acres, known as Rensselaerswyck. His tenant farmers settled along the rich alluvial riverbanks first. Mill, timber, and mineral rights were reserved to the patroon, and these were leased out separately as the needs required. Under such leases, mills appeared

early along the small streams which flowed into the Hudson. Winding Indian trails became the roads inland while the river itself provided much of the transportation for the early communities.

Settlement was concurrent on the east and west sides of the river with farmers in the East Greenbush area from 1631 onward. In 1642 the patroon appointed a pastor, the Rev. Johannes Megapolensis, to establish a Dutch Reformed church for Rensselaerswyck. The parsonage, residences, mills, and a fort were set up in the center of Van Rensselaer's colony on the east side of the river in the area which would become Rensselaer, across from Fort Orange and today's Albany. A ferry connected the two settlements in 1642 and was controlled by the Van Rensselaers until the nineteenth century.

In 1664 the Dutch New Netherlands were surrendered to the English and the colony was renamed New York for King Charles II's brother James, Duke of York and Albany. The small town of Beverwyck on the western bank of the river took on the name of Albany. The English takeover changed little of the actual day-to-day life in the colony. Gov. Thomas Dongan confirmed the Van Rensselaer family's ownership of the Manor of Rensselaerswyck in a charter which extended the manor south of Castleton to a point opposite Coeymans, north to a point opposite Cohoes, and inland on both sides of the river some twenty-four miles. Rensselaer County would later be made out of the eastern portion of this manor, with the addition of a number of smaller patents of land which had been granted to other families along the northern third of the county.

The British skirmishes with the French for supremacy in North America erupted into warfare throughout the mid-1700s. Canadian Indians were allies of the French in this matter and Indian attacks on the scattered settlers were frequent enough to slow down the development of the area. In 1746, Indians murdered six members of the Van Iveren household, about a mile from what is now Defreestville. This and many similar violent incidents from Schaghticoke down to Nassau led John Van Rensselaer to fortify his house, Crailo, and caused many other families to flee from their homes in all outlying areas of the county. Peace came briefly from 1748 to 1755, but the attacks resumed until Provincial and British troops were able to defeat the French, who instigated the attacks, and took over their fort at Crown Point on Lake Champlain in 1759.

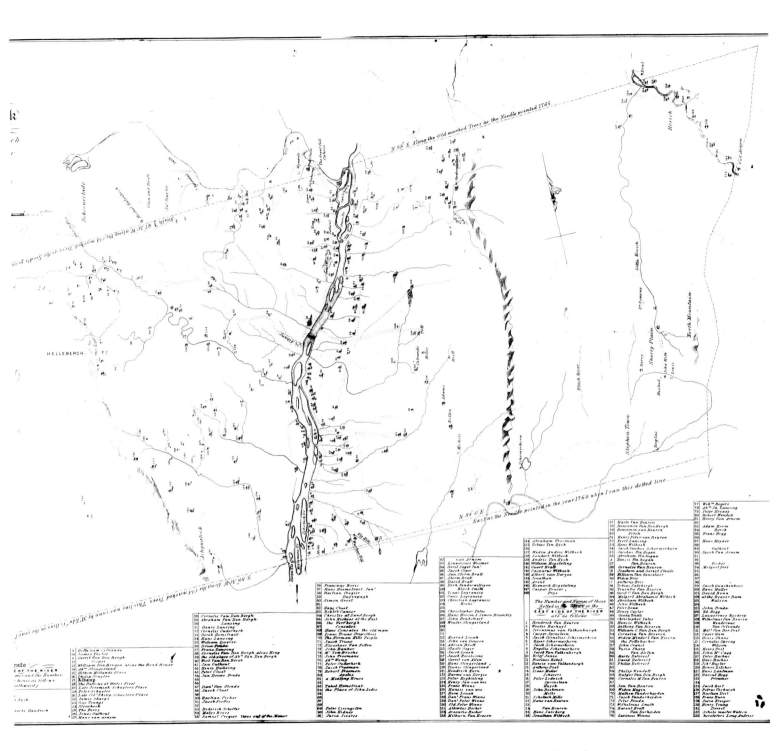

The Manor of Rensselaerswyck was surveyed by John R. Bleeker in 1767, only a few years after the conclusion of the French and Indian Wars had brought peace to the area. By noting the location of each farm, he graphically showed the early pattern of development in Rensselaer County. The earliest and most densely populated areas were the lands along the easily traveled rivers. The Hoosic River was a separate patent of 1688, settled throughout its length as densely as the small piece of it seen here. Small, swiftly flowing streams provided important sources of power as well as routes through the dense forest, while the interior of the county was left wild for about the first hundred years of the colony. *Courtesy of New York State Library Manuscripts and Special Collections*

The assurance of peace opened the county for settlement. Large numbers of New England Yankees, hearing of the opportunities in the area, came westward to settle on farms. Most of the fertile riverfront lands were already taken by the Dutch so these new immigrants began to settle the inland towns and hills. In October 1765, Stephen Van Rensselaer began to lease an enormous tract of twelve thousand acres of land to settlers in the southeastern corner of the county, calling it Stephentown. Settlers from New England soon entered that area, attracted by the rich resources of the land, as well as the opportunities of trade in the growing towns nearby.

The American Revolution slowed down this movement as much of the early fighting against the British centered in the county. Volunteers from towns throughout the county joined the militia to fight. One of the decisive battles of the war, the Battle of Bennington, was fought entirely within the borders of Rensselaer County. Local patriotism was high, especially in Lansingburgh where an association of local residents passed a resolution "never to become slaves" of Great Britain, over a year before the Declaration of Independence was read in Philadelphia.

After the war, settlement continued with renewed vigor. The 1780s and 1790s were a period which saw a number of communities being laid out for development. Lansingburgh was surveyed into lots in 1771, and its success prompted Jacob Vanderheyden to subdivide his own farm to form the town which became Troy. Other early developers surveyed and sold tracts of land in Nassau Village and Castleton. The state legislature chartered the new towns of Hoosick, Pittstown, Schaghticoke, and Stephentown in 1788, giving them the right to be represented in that body. Lansingburgh was incorporated as a village in 1790, the first such village in New York. The county was poised at the edge of coming into its own.

This charming and very early view of the Greenbush area of Rensselaer County from the Albany side of the river was painted by Thomas Davies in 1766. Davies, a young British Army officer, specialized in painting views, some as a military document and others, as is the case with this watercolor, simply as landscape paintings. Other isolated brick farmhouses with tile roofs could be seen farther south on the Hudson River in the early Dutch settlement of Schodack Landing. *Courtesy of Detroit Institute of Arts (56.46) gift of Mrs. George F. Green*

Excavations of Riverside Avenue in Rensselaer along the blocks near Crailo uncovered many artifacts from the seventeenth-century occupants of that area. Indians appeared to have camped on the farm, most likely for trading purposes, and samples of their earthenware were found in addition to Delftware and other European ceramics. Other artifacts, pictured here, included (top to bottom) an iron jew's-harp, a raspberry-style prunt (an applied glass decoration used on seventeenth century Dutch glasses), kaolin pipe stem fragments, pieces of copper, glass bead, and a brass thong tip.

Rensselaer would become famous among musicians in the nineteenth century for J. R. Smith's factory which produced the best jew's-harps in America. Originally from Birmingham, England, Smith moved to Bath-on-Hudson (now part of the city of Rensselaer) and opened his factory. His sons continued the business well into the 1960s. *Courtesy of New York State Office of Parks, Recreation and Historic Preservation, Bureau of Historic Sites*

17

A typical example of the Dutch houses which were at one time common in Rensselaer County, the Hendrik Bries House (variant spelling *Breese*) was built about three miles south of what is today Rensselaer. Legend has it that the house was built in 1722, and the house is noted on Bleecker's 1767 survey map of the east portion of the Manor of Rensselaer-swyck. (Mrs. Bries was by then a widow.) Distinctively Dutch features of the house are its steep pitched roof, bricks laid in a triangular pattern along the roof line (called mouse toothing), and the handsome iron beam-anchors in a trefoil pattern. *Courtesy of Rensselaer County Historical Society*

This well-preserved stone house, listed on the National Register of Historic Places, has been the home of the Staats family for eleven generations, since at least the 1690s. It is located on Papscanee Island, which was purchased from the Mahican Indians in 1637. Also known as Staats Island, this is said to be one of the most productive agricultural sites in the county. A substantial part of the island has been under cultivation for over three hundred years. *Plate from Reynolds,* Dutch Houses; *courtesy of New York State Library Manuscripts and Special Collections*

The lands of Rensselaerswyck were passed on to the firstborn son of each Van Rensselaer patroon, but within that area other members of the family owned large farms. Kiliaen Van Rensselaer, one of many generations to carry the name of the first patroon, built this house for his bride Ariaantje Schuyler in 1742. The house remained in the family until sold at the end of the century to George Clinton, New York State's first governor.

Clinton resold it to his son-in-law, Edmund Charles Genêt, in 1802. Genêt, a French aristocrat who was sent to the United States in 1793 as an envoy, had attempted to get America's support for France in that country's war with Britain. When the United States government refused aid, Genêt went beyond his authority and appealed directly to the American people for help. President Washington asked for his recall, but by 1794 extreme radicals had taken over the French government, and Genêt sought asylum in the United States. He later married Clinton's daughter and remained in East Greenbush for the rest of his life, devoting himself to useful service in the interests of his adopted state and country. *Plate from Reynolds,* Dutch Houses; *courtesy of New York State Library Manuscripts and Special Collections*

Settlement on the east bank of the Hudson River began soon after the first Dutch fort was built on the west bank in what is now Albany. By 1661 Crailo was a well-established farm in the area called Groenen Bosch (Greenbush) for its pine forests. Crailo was named for a Van Rensselaer estate in Holland; it roughly translates to "Crow's Woods."

After 1704 Hendrick Van Rensselaer, younger brother of the patroon, settled in this house. Hendrick's portion of Rensselaerswyck included the 1,500 acre farm called Crailo as well as land in Columbia County known as the Lower Manor.

In later years the farm became an important military headquarters marked on military maps. Hendrick Van Rensselaer's descendants continued to occupy the house, enlarged by the family over the years, until late in the nineteenth century. The building was donated to the state in 1924 by a Van Rensselaer descendant who had rescued it from demolition. It is now a museum whose extensive collections and exhibits focus on all aspects of the Dutch culture and lifestyle along the Hudson River. *Courtesy of Rensselaer County Historical Society*

During the French and Indian Wars, British regulars and colonial militiamen camped on the Crailo farm prior to marching on French forts to the north. The British were amused at the unmilitary appearance of the country recruits, and legend has it that one of their medical officers wrote new verses for an old English tune to make fun of them. The resulting song, "Yankee Doodle," was later adopted by the Colonials as a rallying symbol during the American Revolution. Fifers are said to have played it to the British troops as they surrendered after American victories at Saratoga and Yorktown.

Artist George Gray depicted the creation of "Yankee Doodle" in one of a series of murals he painted in Troy's Hendrick Hudson Hotel in 1937. The mural now hangs in Rensselaer City Hall. *Courtesy of Rensselaer County Historical Society*

In 1771 Abraham J. Lansingh (subsequent generations dropped the "h" from the spelling) had a portion of his farm surveyed and subdivided into streets, alleys, and 288 lots to form the village of Lansingburgh. New settlers quickly moved in and the area began to grow.

Lansingh's original village home was built in 1749 and he lived there after acquiring the Stone Arabia Patent in 1763. Located on the west side of Second Avenue near 110th Street, the building was demolished in 1962 to make room for a new supermarket.

Built about the same time as Lansingh's house, this building is one of several farm-houses which remain from that period before the street grid pattern was first laid out. In fact, First Avenue still has a curve in it to go around the property. In the 1790s, Dr. Aaron Hinman owned it and added a little wooden doctor's office, now attached to the house on the left side. The building still stands with its massive cooking fireplace intact. *Courtesy of Frances D. Broderick*

In 1653 Jacob Vanderheyden, a Dutch tailor, came to New Amsterdam and a year later moved to Albany. In 1707 his son Dirck acquired farmlands on the eastern part of Rensselaerswyck in the area which was later to become Troy. Since the lands lay within the Manor of Rensselaerswyck, he paid the patroon a yearly ground rent of three and three-quarters bushels of wheat and two fat hens. In the ensuing years the property changed hands many times, all within the Vanderheyden family and was ultimately divided into three farms. The commercial success of Lansingburgh to the north prompted Jacob D. Vanderheyden, owner of the middle of the three farms, to divide his sixty-five acres into lots laid out along streets and alleys as in Philadelphia. The planned village was to be called Vanderheyden, but two years later, in 1789, the residents, mostly of English descent, chose the classical name of Troy.

This house belonged to Matthias Vanderheyden and was situated on the corner of River and Division streets. Built in 1752, the house had a typically Dutch gambrel roof like that of the rear extension. In subsequent years the roofline was raised as shown in this 1867 photograph. The building became Ashley's Tavern, a favorite stop for travelers coming from the east in the late 1700s. *Courtesy of Rensselaer County Historical Society*

The Knickerbacker Mansion, now owned by the Knickerbocker Historical Society, sits on a fertile plain not far from the Hoosic River in an area once known as the Witenagemot tract. The property it occupies was originally purchased by Herman Knickerbacker from the Hoosac Indian Chief Soquon in 1707. Knickerbacker first constructed a log home, and around 1770 he completed a handsome brick structure, much modified in the Victorian period. Here Colonial soldiers mustered for the defense of Saratoga during the Revolutionary War, and Lafayette visited during his triumphant return trip to America in 1825.

Sharing the history of the site with the mansion is the tale of the Witenagemot Oak. For many years during the latter half of the 1600s, the northeastern colonies suffered through a long series of bitter wars with the Indians, known as King Philip's Wars. In 1676 a peace treaty was signed here and commemorated with the planting of an oak tree which became known as the Witenagemot Oak. The tree stood at the rear of the Knickerbacker Mansion and lived for 273 years until it was uprooted by the flooding of the Hoosic River. *Jim Shaughnessy photo; courtesy of the photographer*

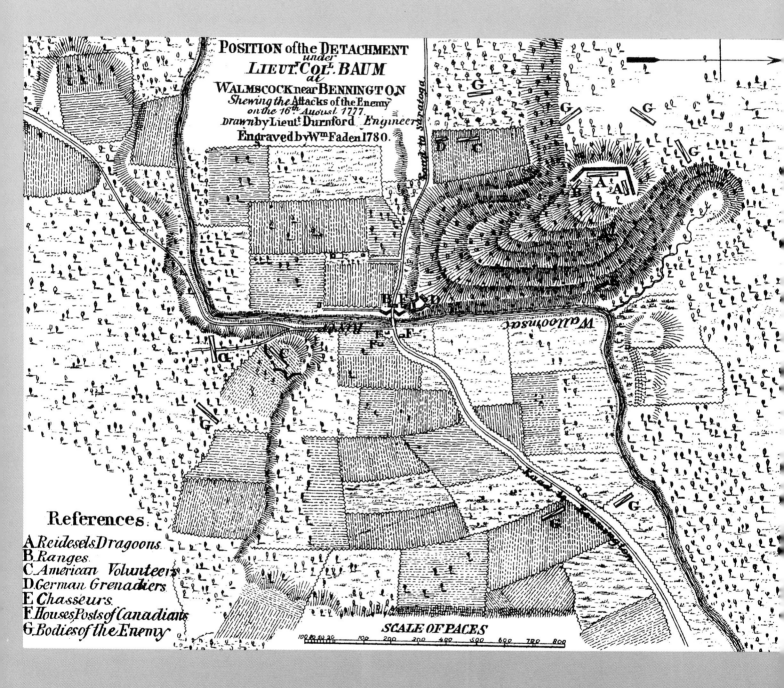

POSITION of the DETACHMENT
under
LIEUT. COLE. BAUM
at
WALMSCOCK near BENNINGTON
Shewing the Attacks of the Enemy
on the 16th August 1777.
drawn by Lieut. Durnford Engineer
Engraved by Wm Faden 1780.

References:

A. *Reidesels Dragoons.*
B. *Ranges.*
C. *American Volunteers.*
D. *German Grenadiers.*
E. *Chasseurs.*
F. *Houses Posts of Canadians.*
G. *Bodies of the Enemy.*

SCALE OF PACES
100 80 60 40 20   100   200   300   400   500   600   700   800

In the first year of the American Revolution, a major goal of the British generals was to link their forces in Canada and New York City along the natural roadways of the Hudson and Mohawk River valleys. As Gen. John Burgoyne marched his forces southward from Canada, fleeing Colonials burned crops and blocked roads before him. By August 1777, supplies were badly needed by British troops. Hearing of a large store of American supplies in Bennington, Vermont, General Burgoyne sent German mercenaries to seize them. Local settlers rushed to join the American forces at Bennington. On August 16, 1777, American militiamen under the command of Gen. John Stark fought and defeated the Germans at Walloomsac in the town of Hoosick. After the battle, this map was prepared for General Burgoyne to show the location of the different regiments as the Americans attacked.

Cheered by their victory at Walloomsac, many of the Colonials went on to join the American forces then assembling at Saratoga. Called the "turning point of the Revolution," that decisive battle in October 1777 ended with the defeat of General Burgoyne and the end of major Revolutionary War activity in this area.

In the early years of this century, Battlefield Park, site of the battle, was a popular stop for picnics and sightseeing on the Hoosick Falls and Walloomsac Street Railway. Today the park is a state historic site where visitors can look out over the fields where American militiamen first crushed the British hopes of dividing the colonies. *Map from Sylvester,* History; *photo courtesy of New York State Office of Parks, Recreation and Historic Preservation*

These log cabins in Berlin, were photographed by J. F. Cowee. *Courtesy of
Rensselaer County Historical Society*

Chapter Two

1791-1825
A County Is Born

The signing of a peace treaty with Great Britain in 1783 signaled the end of war and the beginning of a new nation. As the new government was reorganized, many of New York's original county boundaries were also changed. The rapid growth of settlements on the eastern side of the Hudson River warranted the separation of that portion of Albany County, so on February 7, 1791, Rensselaer County was established by the State Legislature. Both Troy and Lansingburgh sought to become the new county seat, but Troy's citizens won the honor by virtue of pledging all the money necessary to build the new public buildings as well as donating the land.

Continued immigration and growth led to the establishment of new towns within Rensselaer County. Petersburg was created from parts of Stephentown in 1791, Greenbush was incorporated in 1792, Schodack in 1795. Stephentown was further divided in 1806 to form Berlin and Nassau, and the following year saw the establishment of both Brunswick and Grafton. Sand Lake was created in 1812.

The renewal of war with England in 1812 made an army outpost along the northern routes to Lake Champlain important once again, along with the need for readily available munitions and supplies. The American Army made its headquarters in a cantonment at East Greenbush, and the farms and factories of Rensselaer County supplied its many needs.

More than 80 percent of the population was supported by farming at this time, and the importance of agriculture was underlined by early newspapers such as Troy's 1797 *Farmers' Oracle* and Lansingburgh's *Farmers Register,* as well as by the establishment of county agricultural societies and fairs. Local industries were most often based on the processing of farm and forest products in gristmills, sawmills, cheese factories, tanneries, flouring mills, malt factories, breweries, and cider mills—all powered by the many fast-flowing streams and waterfalls of the county.

Improved transportation routes were essential to the expansion of trade and commerce. Sloops and other vessels sailed the Hudson River from ports such as Lansingburgh and Castleton-on-Hudson south to New York City in a matter of days, and by 1825 a number of steamboats were making the trip overnight. Inland roads, many following Indian trails and riverbeds, improved with the establishment of turnpike associations to lay out and maintain new roads.

Construction of the Erie and Champlain canals brought new immigrants to the area and opened up the interior of the state for commerce. Troy's merchants were not slow to take advantage of this. The first load of goods to travel west on the Erie Canal on the day it opened, October 8, 1823, was on the *Trojan Trader,* bound for Rochester.

As early as 1780 vessels were being built in Lansingburgh for the ocean and river trade. Many were used in the West Indies trade, bringing back rum, molasses, and sugar. Locally constructed sloops, schooners, scows, and other boats were purchased by industrialists to bring in raw materials and ship out the products of riverfront factories.

Because the Hudson River was so vital to village livelihoods, Lansingburgh newspapers routinely reported what ships were in port, for sale, or lost at sea, who won the regatta, and what ice conditions were. Federal laws required owners to enroll ships at designated regional ports by name and shipyard of origin. Since this same information was required of each subsequent owner, these enrollments, many still in existence, are particularly useful in researching the shipbuilding industry.

The sloop *Wasp* was one of several ships built in Lansingburgh which served the United States in the War of 1812. In later years it served as a stone sloop, carrying up to one hundred tons of rock at a time. It is shown here in the late 1800s, carrying a load of granite up the Indian River in Connecticut. The sloop was abandoned in 1902. *Print from original painting by Victor Mays; courtesy of Frances D. Broderick*

The Waterford bridge was completed in 1804 under the direction of celebrated bridge architect and builder Theodore Burr of Oxford, New York. A four-span toll bridge with a double roadway, it was built of hand-hewn white and red pine, and featured an ingenious structural design consisting of wooden arches strengthened by trusses. The cost of constructing the covered bridge was fifty thousand dollars.

Local historians tell the story of one of the first gatekeepers on the bridge, Joseph Sturges, who sold gingerbread and small beer at his station on the Lansingburgh end and never allowed a person to cross without paying his toll. Apparently, during the War of 1812, General Bloomfield arrived at the Lansingburgh gate with three thousand men and numerous wagons and artillery pieces. Sturges demanded the standard toll of three cents for each man and eighteen cents for each vehicle and refused to let them cross. Only after the general threatened to blow up the toll gate did Sturges finally let them by.

In 1834 the Rensselaer and Saratoga Railroad wanted to use the bridge for its new line from Troy, but objections from local citizens forced them to build the 1,512 feet long Green Island bridge instead. Later adapted for use by trolley cars, the Waterford bridge had stood for more than one hundred years when it caught fire in July 1909.

Bystanders and boaters watched futilely as

the bridge's sides and roof burned away, exposing the underlying structural system which soon fell to the flames. Its replacement a four-span steel bridge, utilizes the same piers, newly reinforced, and is still in use after rehabilitation in 1984. A similar wooden covered bridge built in 1801 still exists over the Hoosic River at Buskirk. It is perhaps the oldest bridge standing in the county today.
Courtesy of Rensselaer County Historical Society

An early road along the river above Lansingburgh provided a scenic buggy ride for these travelers. Road transportation in Rensselaer County was greatly improved by turnpike companies begun in the 1790s. Groups of investors set up the companies and then charged travelers tolls to cover the costs of building and maintaining the roads. Turnpikes like the Farmer's, East Greenbush and Hudson, Columbia, Northern, and Troy and Bennington crossed the county and utilized the latest in engineering and surveying practices. Further upgrading was possible due to improvements in road surface technology, such as the development in 1804 of an impervious road surface of tightly bound stones by Thomas Telford and John McAdam (hence, "macadam" pavement). State and local takeover of the early toll roads occurred in the mid-nineteenth century, and the turnpike companies and their tollgates disappeared. *Courtesy of Frances D. Broderick*

The patents first sold to individuals in the seventeenth century established patterns of property lines which remained long after the original owners had passed on. This was especially evident in the northernmost third of Rensselaer County. A large portion of Schaghticoke had been set aside for Indians in 1670. Other lands along the river were part of the Hoosic Patent, with farms laid out perpendicular to the Hoosic River as it curves east and south through the county. Hoosick Falls filled in the northeastern corner of the county while Pittstown, sold in much smaller tracts to individuals, incorporated almost all of the land left in between. By 1829 small communities dotted the countryside and turnpikes laced together the county, following the routes still used by modern highways. Route 7 from Troy to Pittstown was especially known for its new hard surface, and was labeled on maps as simply "McAdamized Road." *Courtesy of E. H. Gemmill*

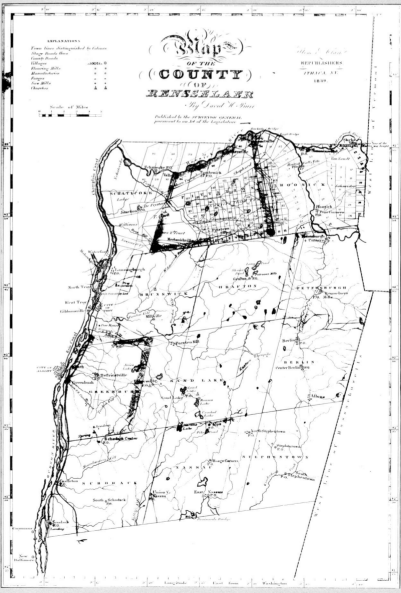

Every town in Rensselaer County had several taverns along the main roads to provide refreshment and lodging for travelers whose average speed might be a dizzying four miles per hour. Taverns often housed the general store and might contain a larger room known as the "ballroom" which was used for dances and other entertainments, as well as meetings. Taverns were often the central gathering place where town business was conducted and elections were held.

Because of their location, innkeepers were important citizens. They were often the first to hear news from outside town in the days before the telegraph, and they met all types of travelers. Salesmen were important clients, as they traveled from town to town by horse and cart with catalogs and sample cases of their wares.

The Lewis Tavern was located at Schodack Center west of the Schodack Town Hall. It was destroyed for highway construction. *Courtesy of Schodack Town Historian*

The Rensselaer Glass Works at Rouse's Lake (now Glass Lake in the town of Sand Lake) was started in 1802. The plant covered almost 150 acres at the lake site and included about five thousand acres of woodland nearby, used to furnish fuel for the glass-making processes. According to recent research, officials of the Glass Works brought glass blowers from Germany and Scotland to work for them. These artisans had to be smuggled out of these countries because they were officially employees of the heads of state. The Germans made cylinder glass and the Scots made crown glass. In 1825, 467 boxes of window glass were made and sold in ten days, valued at 594 pounds or about three thousand dollars. Some glass workers were reported to earn as much as sixty dollars per week—a phenomenal wage for that time. The works had as many as sixty employees during the best times. In 1852, however, a fire devasted the glass works and it was never rebuilt.

The nineteenth century homes of the glass workers and the owners shown in this scene as well as the Hidley painting on the bookjacket are still an attractive feature of present day Glass Lake. *Courtesy of Judy Rowe*

The ice left after a spring flood did not stop trading activity at the Old Mill near Castleton-on-Hudson. This stream and millsite were bought from the Indians in 1648 and soon developed. These buildings date from the early 1800s.

The location of a mill next to its source of power meant taking a chance that the stream would overflow its banks. Mills along the Poestenkill in Troy were swept away during a hurricane in 1938, and the Little Hoosic in 1979 caused a spring flood in Berlin. The Kinderhook flooded Stephentown that same year, as did the Quackenkill in Clum's Corners. *Courtesy of Schodack Town Historian*

UNCLE SAM WILSON OF TROY SUPPLIED BEEF TO THE UNITED STATES ARMY DURING THE WAR OF 1812 – STAMPING HIS BARRELS WITH THE LETTERS *"U.S."* – THIS BEEF BECAME KNOWN TO THE ARMY AS *"UNCLE SAM'S"* AND THIS FAMILIAR APPELLATION WAS THEREAFTER BESTOWED ON OUR OWN GOVERNMENT ★ ★ ★

The War of 1812 between England and the United States had a direct impact on those states which lay closest to the northern borders. American troops preparing for the Canadian campaign were stationed in barracks in Greenbush, and local merchants received important contracts for the provision of supplies. Samuel Wilson, owner of a meatpacking firm in Troy, supplied beef for the troops. As was customary in those days, the meat was packed in wooden barrels stamped *E.A.* for the government purchasing

agent (Elbert Anderson), and *U.S.* for the purchaser (United States). According to one version of the story, however, Wilson's workers joked that the *U.S.* stood for Uncle Sam, their nickname for their boss. As the joke spread from local workers to the soldiers quartered at Greenbush, then transferred elsewhere, all government-stamped goods came to be called "Uncle Sam's." Eventually a cartoon figure was created to symbolize the United States.

A mural of Uncle Sam Wilson overseeing a

delivery of beef to the cantonment was painted by George Gray for the Hendrick Hudson Hotel in Troy. It is now owned by the Rensselaer County Historical Society. The long tradition of slaughterhouses and meatpackers which dotted the countrysides and clustered in the cities is carried on today by companies such as Levonian, Helmbold and Troy Park. *Courtesy of Rensselaer County Historical Society*

The cantonment at Greenbush was a large army camp of about three hundred acres which could quarter up to four thousand soldiers during the War of 1812. The troops slept in tents, but there were eight officers' barracks surrounding the parade grounds. In 1831 the property was sold and the land was used for farming. Beginning in about 1928, most of the land became the site of the Hampton Manor development. Still remaining is one of the officers' barracks near the present Red Mill School. This 1975 photo shows the restored building which now is an apartment house. *Courtesy of Rensselaer County Historical Society*

Brush manufacturing started in Lansingburgh with David McMurray's factory in 1818; two of his sons, William and John, also opened factories there. Although they operated only three of the thirteen brush factories listed in an 1845 New York State census for Lansingburgh, John McMurray's factory was reported to be the largest in the world. By the late 1800s, thirty-five factories were operating in the area and at one time eight hundred people were employed in Lansingburgh's brush-making industry, earning a total of $350,000 in a year. A number of these employees were women who worked at home "drawing brushes."

Bristles were bought by the manufacturers from local farmers, and some of the brush blocks and handles were manufactured in Grafton and Rock Hollow (Brunswick). Exotic woods and inlays were also used in the Lansingburgh brushes, which were known throughout the United States for their quality and beauty.

Here are workers at the brush-making machines in the Monarch Brush Shop, 653 Third Avenue, in Lansingburgh. *Courtesy of Frances D. Broderick*

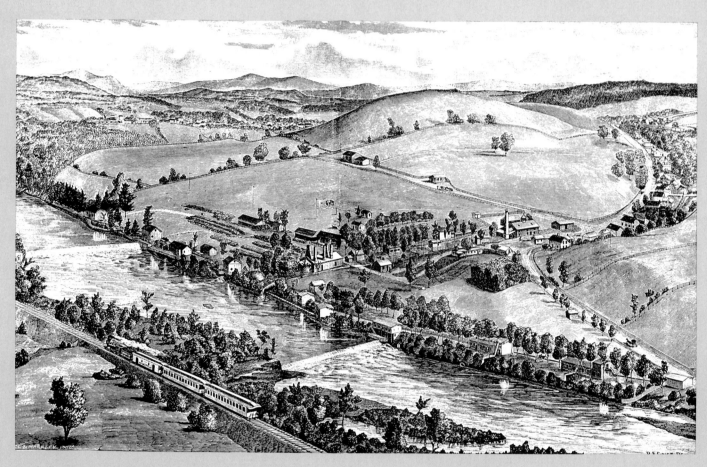

Just before the War of 1812, President Madison requested that New York's governor establish a munitions plant in the upper Hudson Valley accessible to military roads leading to the Canadian border. By 1813, Josiah and Nicholas Masters were supplying gunpowder to the United States troops stationed along the northern borders of New York State. Initially located at Schaghticoke Hill, the mills were moved to the south bank of the Hoosic River near Valley Falls by the 1850s and incorporated as the Schaghticoke Powder Company. Production reached 3,600 pounds per day during the Civil War, and in 1895 the plant produced 1.5 million pounds of powder.

The production of explosives was of necessity a dangerous business and three generations of local residents learned to live with the periodic explosions which broke windows and sent crockery flying. The year 1928 marked the final explosion at the powder plant, however, and the company, then known as the Hercules Powder Company, closed soon thereafter. At least twenty-nine workers, including the four killed that day, lost their lives in explosions during the 115 years of the powder plant's operation. *Courtesy of Richard Lohnes*

Leading citizens heartily supported Rensselaer County's Agricultural Society, organized in 1819 with representatives from each county town. This membership certificate was issued to Ziba Hewit, Grafton's manager. The first Rensselaer County Agricultural Fair was held October 12 and 13 of that same year. Pealing church bells and booming cannon set the stage for a procession from the Court House to the Common at Hoosick and River streets.

There were prize animals on exhibit, a plowing contest won by farmers Filkin and Harrington, an honor guard from the Arsenal, and an elaborate church service, all preceded by an address from the renowned Elkanah Watson, Esq. A champion of improved farming methods, Watson was the organizer of America's first county fair in Berkshire County, Massachusetts in 1810. *Courtesy of Judy Rowe*

Rensselaer County has much in common with other parts of eastern New York in the history of its schools. The early Dutch settlers placed a strong emphasis on education and made it available to all children, male or female. The first teacher was frequently a clergyman, and while parents who could contribute did so, children of the poor were allowed to attend free of charge. The first schools in Rensselaerwyck Manor were set up in the 1650s. While these were not public in the modern sense because of their religious sponsorship and tuition fees, they were a step in that direction.

Not until 1784 when the Board of Regents was set up was there an original plan for state education. General state aid was instituted in 1795 and in 1805 a Common School Fund was established with proceeds from the sale of state lands. Soon all of the towns in the county set up district schools, their numbers varying over the years as the needs changed. An early record of this being done can be seen in a handwritten account of the first district school in Stephentown, which gives numbers of pupils, expenditures, and other information from 1815 to 1839. *Courtesy of Stephentown Town Historian*

Incorporated in 1795, the first Lansingburgh Academy building faced the village green. In 1820 the school moved to 114th Street and Seventh Avenue where this structure was built. Herman Melville and Chester Arthur were among the students. Chester Arthur became a teacher and taught at a number of schools throughout the county. Lansingburgh Academy students could choose from a wide variety of science and mathematics courses. The 1820 building is still in use; it contains several classrooms and a branch of the public library. *Courtesy of Frances D. Broderick*

The beloved Christmas poem, "A Visit from St. Nicholas," was first published in the now extinct newspaper the *Troy Sentinel* on December 23, 1823. More commonly known by its first line, "T'was the night before Christmas," it was the creation of an Episcopal priest and theological scholar in New York City, Rev. Clement C. Moore, who was a good friend of the rector of St. Paul's Episcopal Church in Troy, Rev. David Butler. Butler's daughter first heard the poem on a visit to the Moore family and persuaded the Troy paper to publish it. For many years, the author remained anonymous, as Reverend Moore feared that his children's Christmas treat would seem too frivolous for such a distinguished scholar as he.

One of the many artists to illustrate the poem was Grandma Moses, well-known primitive painter. Her home for over fifty years was near Eagle Bridge, and many of her paintings depict rural scenes in Rensselaer County. *Grandma Moses:* Santa Claus I. *Copyright 1973, Grandma Moses Properties Co., New York*

Built in 1840 on a plateau north of Rensselaer, the Beverwyck Manor House was intended to serve as the center of the East Manor by William P. Van Rensselaer, who had inherited that half of Rensselaerswyck. He lived there only a few years, however, before selling the estate to Paul S. Forbes from New York City, whose family used it primarily as a summer residence. Some historians consider the house to be the work of Albany architect Philip Hooker, and the grounds are reputed to have been designed by noted landscape architect Andrew Jackson Downing. The building is listed on the National Register of Historic Places. Today the building is owned by the Franciscan brotherhood, who recently celebrated the seventy-fifth anniversary of their use of the house as a seminary. *Courtesy of New York State Library Manuscripts and Special Collections*

Navigation on the Hudson River immediately above Troy was greatly improved by constructing a combined dam and sloop lock. The original dam and lock, completed in 1823, was located opposite Middleburgh Street, one block south of the present Federal Dam. A hydraulic canal branched off the river above the dam and was used for power by several industries below the dam, including William Connors's Paint Manufacturing Company. By the beginning of the twentieth century the early dam and lock shown here appeared primitive and worn out, as evidenced by the makeshift ladders, and leaking lock gates.

In 1903 New York State voters passed a $101 million referendum for a new barge canal system. The federal government started a new dam in 1913, which included a new concrete dam and a 45 feet by 520 feet lock. At a cost of $1.5 million it opened in August 1915. Shortly thereafter the old dam was dynamited. *Courtesy of Rensselaer County Historical Society*

The burgeoning of facilities for common schools was accompanied by the inauguration of institutions for higher education. It is significant that two of the best known Rensselaer County institutions, the Troy Female Seminary and Rensselaer Polytechnic Institute, began at about the same time. The primary shapers of both, Emma Willard and Amos Eaton, were associated with each other in their academic endeavors.

In 1821, Emma Willard opened the county's first school for girls, the Troy Female Seminary, at the invitation of Troy's prominent citizens. The school began with ninety students from New York and at least seven other states gathering for classes in Moulton's Coffeehouse on Congress and Second streets. In 1830 the buildings pictured here replaced the old on the original site.

Not only was Emma Willard a pioneer in women's education, but she also espoused the necessity for females to be trained in science and mathematics at a time when it was widely believed the female mind could not withstand such rigorous exercise. Students at Troy Female Seminary studied geology, physics, and higher math, in addition to the courses in art, music, and French more usually offered to girls. Emma's sister, Almira, joined her in 1824 and worked closely with Amos Eaton of RPI in teaching science. Almira published a series of lectures on botany which went into nine editions and sold 275,000 copies by 1872.

Emma Willard also pioneered the preparation of teachers. To any student who agreed to become a teacher she extended credit—the debt to be paid from her future earnings. What soon developed was a teacher placement agency with Emma Willard's signature as the mark of teacher certification.

Pictured here are Emma Willard, the seminary campus in the 1890s, and an early physics lab. *Courtesy of Emma Willard School Archives and Rensselaer County Historical Society*

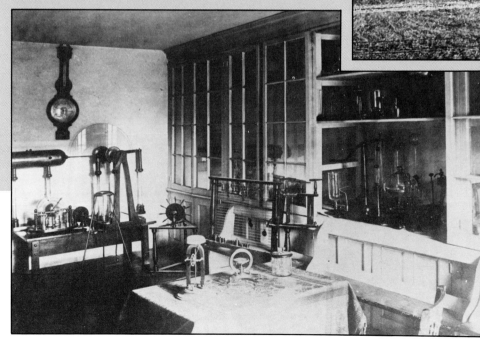

In 1824 Stephen Van Rensselaer established the Rensselaer Institute to teach men "how to put science to practical use." The school was first located in the former Farmer's Bank building on the corner of Middleburgh and River streets near the old state dam in Troy.

Amos Eaton was appointed senior professor, and until his death in 1842, Eaton devoted himself to the institution and to scientific study and publication. It was under Eaton's aegis that the school instituted a "ladies department" in 1834. Directed by a former student at the Troy Female Seminary, it lasted one year with eight young women.

In 1847 the new president, Benjamin F. Greene, began to call the school Rensselaer Polytechnic Institute, and the name was formally legalized by the state legislature in 1861. Green also reorganized the school from a one-year to a three-year program.

Pictured here are Amos Eaton and the original RPI building which no longer stands. *Courtesy of Rensselaer Polytechnic Institute Archives*

This view of the mills along the Poestenkill at Troy includes Griswold Wire Works in the foreground, and (left to right) Thompkins Brothers Machine Works, J. A. Manning Paper Company, and Mount Ida Cotton Factory (later Wultex)—all of which utilized the water power of the Poestenkill Falls. *Courtesy of Rensselaer County Historical Society*

Chapter Three

1826-1860
Expansion And Growth

I n the second quarter of the nineteenth century, Rensselaer County's already rapid growth and development accelerated. Continued improvements in transportation systems opened local factories to national markets and resources. The Erie Canal, completed in 1825, was so heavily used that people were calling for substantial enlargements within the decade. The preeminence of the canals was soon threatened, however, by the advent of the railroad. The Rensselaer and Saratoga Railroad brought the first train to Troy in 1835 and other lines soon followed. The railroad did not actually supplant the waterways for thirty to forty years, and in the meantime, the canals and railways together placed Rensselaer County in the center of a vast transportation network.

While manufacturing concentrated in the vicinity of Troy and Lansingburgh, small factories could be found in every town in the county. The company founded by Walter A. Wood in 1852 in Hoosick Falls, in fact, could rival the largest of Troy's industries. An incredible variety of products came out of the county: horseshoes, bells, cast iron stoves and storefronts, floorcloths, paper, sheet steel, roofing, bricks, leather goods, brushes, currycombs, clothing and textiles of all kinds, twine, whiskey, beer, and much more.

In more urban areas, services expanded to meet new needs and fill new demands. Troy constructed its first public water reservoir in 1832, and by 1848, gas illumination was also available throughout the city. Two years earlier, the first telegraph lines amazed local citizens with almost instantaneous communication with such distant places as Boston and Buffalo. Distances seemed ever smaller.

As county seat, Troy grew rapidly. Its population of 5,268 citizens in 1820 had more than doubled by 1830 and was almost four times as large in 1840. Irish immigrants escaping their country's potato famine flocked to the area, as did immigrants from England, Scotland, and northern Europe. Local Democrats wooed the new citizens and with the help of their votes, took over Troy politics.

New farmlands were settled in the eastern hills of the county as the demand for their farm and forest products grew. Tenant farmers' inability to own their land under the manorial system, still in effect almost two hundred years after such feudal systems had disappeared from Europe, finally exploded into riots in 1839 when the heirs of Stephen Van Rensselaer, "The Good Patroon," sought to collect back rents on his land. Dr. Smith Boughton, resident of Alps, was the leader of this movement which occurred throughout Albany and Rensselaer counties. Only in 1846 was the issue resolved when the new state constitution outlawed the patroon system of land leases.

The county's growing commercial success found reflection in the establishment of fine educational, as well as cultural, institutions. Determined to be a leader in the nation, Rensselaer County set about training her next generation.

Grafton's Prussian Blue factory produced blue dye for more than a century from a formula which was a well-kept secret. In the early 1800s Samuel Davis arrived in the area from New England and found the site on the Quackenkill ideally suited for manufacturing the blue dye. It had ample resources of crystal-clear running water and seemingly infinite forests of red oak for potash, apparently a key ingredient of the formula. Davis purchased the site, and he and his descendants profited from producing and selling the dye.

In its day the dye was shipped by the hogshead throughout the United States and abroad. It was used in dying the fabrics for Civil War uniforms, as a paint whitening agent, and an ingredient of patent leather.

Eventually the forest resources were exhausted, and Davis turned to potassium ferrocyanide from Germany. World War I effectively closed off this source, and by then the technology of dye chemistry had outdistanced the Prussian Blue factory on the Quackenkill. The factory is gone today, but one can still find stones dyed blue on the site. *Courtesy of Brunswick Town Historian*

OIL-CLOTHS

Of a Superior Quality, suitable for

TABLE SPREADS, STOVE, HALL,

& CHAISE CARPETING,

NOW ON HAND.

ORNAMENTAL WORK,

Of the same kind, done in the neatest man-

ner, and after any pattern, by

WILLIAM POWERS.

LANSINGBURGH, *June* 10, 1817.

Manufacturing stoneware pottery was a major early industry in the greater Troy area. Local clay was used as slip to line the pots while ironstone clay used for the exterior was brought upriver from Long Island and New Jersey. The opening of the Erie Canal provided easy access to western markets. Used to store food in the days before refrigeration and plastic containers, they are now highly prized by collectors.

These pots are typical of the work done by George Lent who manufactured pottery in Lansingburgh from 1825 through the 1840s. His kiln was on the west side of Second Avenue, just north of 112th Street, site of a service station today. *Gene Baxter photo; courtesy of Frances D. Broderick*

Oilcloth, produced in Lansingburgh by the Powers as well as the Whipple and Haskell factories, was primarily used as a floor covering, a forerunner of linoleum. When William Powers was killed in an explosion at the factory in 1829, Deborah Ball Powers continued the thriving oilcloth manufacturing business they had started in 1817. As D. Powers and Sons, the firm flourished, adding a Newburgh factory, a New York City warehouse, a sloop, and in 1877, the Bank of D. Powers and Sons. Mrs. Powers, a philanthropist as well as a remarkable business woman, established the Deborah Powers Home for Aged Ladies late in her life. Across the street from the Powers Home at 415 Second Avenue, she also began a park as a memorial to her husband, which still exists today. *Courtesy of Rensselaer County Historical Society*

A Rensselaer County gazetteer of 1840 describes the hamlet of Poestenkill as having one hundred people, twenty dwelling houses, a Lutheran church, a Dutch Reformed church, two taverns, two stores, two factories, a gristmill, and a sawmill. Mills were important for processing agricultural products and often provided the first economic stimulus for a community's growth.

Located on the pond which provided its waterpower, this mill produced cider, lumber, and many kinds of flour and feed through the first half of the twentieth century. One of its specialties, however, was fine buckwheat flour, sifted through silk sieves.

Through the years the owners of the gristmill shown here have included Christian Cooper, Coonradt C. Cooper, George Cooper, Leonard Lynd, F. B. Taylor, John W. Holser, and Albert J. Schumann. As late as 1945, the mill was operated by Sanford Catlin, a Poestenkill native who now has his own sawmill. The mill was demolished around 1950, but the mill pond still provides the swimming and skating of years gone by. *Courtesy of Poestenkill Bicentennial Commission*

WALTER A. WOOD'S
IMPROVED FOLDING BAR MOWER.
WALTER A. WOOD'S
IMPROVED SELF-RAKING REAPER
WALTER A. WOOD'S
Improved Self-Raking Reaper and Mower Combined!

The highest prizes ever offered on Harvesting Machines have been awarded these Machines, in England, France and America. Among them,

TWO GRAND GOLD MEDALS!
AND THE
Grand Cross of the Legion of Honor!
AT THE
GREAT PARIS EXPOSITION AND FIELD TRIAL IN 1867

Together with more than two hundred first-class County, District and State Prizes. Over one hundred and twenty-one thousand of these Machines have been made and sold.

For lightness of draught, simplicity of construction, durability, ease of management, and perfection of work, these Machines excel all others.

For sale through our agents all over the world. Descriptive Circulars will be sent *free*, on application to the Manufacturers. Manufactured by

WALTER A. WOOD
Mowing and Reaping Machine Company, - HOOSICK FALLS, N. Y.

Iron-making in Rensselaer County had its beginnings about 1807 when two small iron plants were erected on the Wynantskill. The financial capital for these early iron works came from Albany, but the power sites were in Troy, where the Wynantskill tumbles two hundred feet to the Hudson River.

Henry Burden arrived from Scotland with a recommendation from the U. S. Minister in Britain. A brilliant inventor and business manager, he became superintendent of the Troy Iron and Nail Factory in 1822, and twenty-six years later was full owner. Burden's famous invention of a machine to manufacture horseshoes made Troy the horseshoe capital of the nation and of the world. A single machine was capable of turning out thirty-six hundred horseshoes per hour! The factory reached its greatest capacity when Burden designed and installed a sixty-foot

diameter overshot wheel within the plant (to the rear of the smokestack in this circa 1885 view). In 1862 the Burden Company began to build a new Lower Works along the Hudson River shore just below the Upper Works site; the Upper Works were closed down by 1899.

Even in its decaying state long after the death of its designer and the demolition of the surrounding iron works, the famous water wheel attracted curious sightseers and was much studied by engineers. It finally collapsed in 1914 and was eventually scrapped. The entire site is now wooded with few traces of the once giant industry that existed there.

Overlooking the Wynantskill factory and Burden's home on the distant hill is Woodside Presbyterian Church, still in use today, built in memory of Burden's wife, Helen, in 1869. *Illustration from Proudfit,* Burden; *courtesy of Rensselaer County Historical Society*

The "good years" for New York State farmers were 1850 to 1870. Factories sprang up across the Empire State—then foremost in both agriculture and manufacturing—to meet the new demand for farm machinery. Hoosick Falls, a seat of water-powered industry since the eighteenth century, was home to one of the greatest of these, the Walter A. Wood Mowing and Reaping Machine Company.

Walter A. Wood was an inventor as well as a manufacturer and entrepreneur. He learned machining skills as an apprentice to his father, who manufactured plows. By 1850

Wood had started manufacturing a reaper in Hoosick Falls. He continued to add to his line and his facilities, producing an average of five thousand machines per year by 1860. In that year, fire destroyed the burgeoning factory complex, but Wood employees were soon back at work in new, improved facilities. With sales offices in both Europe and the United States, the company shipped thousands of machines annually, and the names Wood and Hoosick Falls were known to farmers and farm machinery dealers around the world. *Courtesy of G. Steven and Stacy P. Draper*

Haying was one of the industries upon which the farmer depended for cash. Tons of hay were taken to the cities for bedding for the many horses, and many more tons were made into bales at the hay presses in the river towns to be shipped to New York. Rye straw was used as insulation in the ice houses found in every town, hamlet, and on most farms. This scene is in Grafton. *Elmer Jacobs photo; courtesy of Rensselaer County Historical Society*

Brunswick's fine agricultural lands, which attracted substantial settlement in the eighteenth century, flourished in the course of the nineteenth century. Potatoes were one important crop—by 1872, 150,000 barrels were shipped to New York—and Brunswick hay also helped support the city's vast number of horses. Many local farmers had routes in Troy, as well, where they peddled eggs, milk, vegetables, fruits and cordwood well into the present century. Milk, eggs, and poultry are now the primary products of the many farms whose silos still dot the rolling Brunswick landscape.

As the farmers prospered, they often remodeled or rebuilt their first small farmhouses in the majestic Greek Revival style popular in this country from the 1830s to 1850s. Houses similar to the Collyson farm can be seen throughout rural areas of New York State. Among Brunswick's earliest farmers were German Palatines who settled in the Haynerville area in the late 1740s. The church they founded, now known as the Gilead Lutheran Church, is still active today. *Courtesy of Brunswick Town Historian*

ATTENTION! ANTI-RENTERS!

AWAKE! AROUSE!

A Meeting of the friends of Equal Rights will be held on *July 4th* *Hoag's Corners* in the Town of *Nassau* at *12* O'clock.

Let the opponents of Patroonry rally in their strength. A great crisis is approaching. Now is the time to strike. The minions of Patroonry are at work. No time is to be lost. Awake! Arouse! and

Strike 'till the last armed foe expires,
Strike for your altars and your fires—
Strike for the green graves of your sires,
God and your happy homes!

☞ The Meeting will be addressed by PETER FINKLE and other Speakers.

After the American Revolution, Stephen Van Rensselaer, descendant of the first patroon, leased much of his land to New England farmers migrating into the area. His terms were easy and he often failed to collect the rent, earning him the title, "The Good Patroon." When he died in 1839, his sons began to collect back rents to pay estate debts from thousands of tenant farmers who lived on the Van Rensselaer manor. Those lands embraced most of what are now Albany and Rensselaer counties and part of Columbia County. Many farmers refused to pay, and the Van Rensselaer heirs resorted to the county sheriffs and courts.

The Anti-Rent Wars ensued, involving among others many Rensselaer County farmers and men of principle who were both angry and determined. Dr. Smith Boughton of Alps, in the town of Nassau, was a primary leader and major centers of resistance were in Hoag's Corners near Boughton's home, and in Grafton. Each year now, the citizens of Hoag's Corners commemorate the struggle with a reenactment on the Fourth of July. *Courtesy of New York State Museum*

The Hudson River Valley has remained a major transportation route in America, from well before the time of the first settlers. It was through the Hudson and Mohawk valleys that New York State held an advantage over all the other states—a level route to the Great Lakes and the West through the Appalachian barrier. Prior to 1750, American colonists were primarily dependent upon water transportation. Christopher Colles, a well-known road surveyor, published a book of road maps in 1789 which included a road from what is now Rensselaer to New York. This road later became the Farmer's Turnpike. By 1810 there were more than two hundred sloops on the Hudson; by 1850, despite the advent of steam, there were close to five hundred vessels sailing between Albany and New York. In 1851 the Hudson River Railroad from Rensselaer and Troy was completed to New York. The line became part of the New York Central's famous four-track "water level route" from New York to Chicago. The railroad with its speed and all-weather efficiency would come to dominate in the Hudson Valley.

Beer's *Atlas* in 1876 included the P. G. Ten Eyck House in Schodack Landing with the railroad and the river in front. Passenger trains continue in front of the old Dutch house today at speeds of nearly one hundred miles per hour along newly refurbished track on their way to and from New York. *Courtesy of Rensselaer County Historical Society*

As Troy continued to prosper, its streets became lined by fine homes. This view of 59 Second Street shows the house around 1886 at the end of the Hart family's term of residence. The house was built in 1827 as a wedding gift for Betsey and Richard Hart from her father, William Howard. He had John Colegrove, a builder, sent up from New York City to construct the late Federal-style marble house on Second Street which quickly became a local landmark. The property included large gardens (behind the brick wall in the photo), a laundry building, and a carriage house. The Harts added a rear wing to the house in 1836-37.

In 1892 the George Cluett family purchased the house and sold the garden lot to Mrs. Cluett's cousin who quickly built his own elegant residence. The Cluetts added a second addition to the back of 59 Second Street for a modern kitchen and additional space. The George Cluetts gave the house to Albert Cluett, George's nephew, and it was at this point that many of the Colonial Revival details were added to the interior. Albert Cluett left the mansion to the Rensselaer County Historical Society at his death in 1952 and the building has been occupied by the Society's museum, library, and offices ever since. *Courtesy of Rensselaer County Historical Society*

At the corner of Fifth Avenue and Fulton Street stands the W. and L. E. Gurley Company. Founded in 1845 as Phelps and Gurley (the name was officially changed in 1852), the company manufactures surveying and mathematical instruments known throughout the world for their quality. This building was designed and built in a matter of six months after the fire of 1862.

The firm was a leader in the manufacture of precise weights and measures, stream gauging, meteorological, and paper testing instruments. During World War II, special photographic patterns were produced on glass for artillery use which led to the development of optical photoelectric rotary and linear measuring instruments for many types of industries. In 1968 the firm was purchased by Teledyne, Inc. now known as Teledyne Gurley, the company makes electronic measuring instruments. *Courtesy of Rensselaer County Historical Society*

TROY MUSEUM

W. H. MEEKER, ------ Manager.

This is the only regular place of public amusement in the city, and is open daily, from 8 o'clock A. M., to 10 P. M.

The Entertainments in the Lecture Room, are by a Company heretofore unequalled in this city in numbers and ability, and being changed every evening, present a series of attractions well worthy the attention of both strangers and citizens.

Increased Attraction !!

Bulwer's Great Play of the

LADY OF LYONS

For one Night only !!

Thursday Evening, Sept. 19, 1850,

Will be presented the first time this season, Bulwer's
Celebrated Play of the

LADY OF LYONS !!

or,

LOVE AND PRIDE.

Fancy Dance, by

MAD'LLE THEODORE.

COMIC SONG, BY

MR. LEFFINGWELL.

To conclude with the Laughable Farce of

POPPING THE QUESTION!!

In Rehearsal, the *Bride* of *Abydos*, from Lord Byron's Poem of that name.

Admission 25 cents.   Children half price.

Boys to the Gallery, half price. - - - *Box Seats* 12 1-2 *cents extra*. Arm Chairs in the Orchestra, 25 cents extra.

Seats can be engaged during the day at the Museum office

Doors open at 6 1-2. - - - - *Curtain will rise at* 7 1-2.

Johnson & Davis, Printers, Cannon Place, Troy.

Living in the city held the advantage of more frequent theater performances. The Troy Museum at State and River streets was comparable to Barnum's Museum in New York City with its daytime exhibitions of stuffed animals, rocks, fossils, gems, and art, both early and contemporary. At Saturday matinees there would be plays for the young folk. In the mid-nineteenth century with its prominent place as a crossroads of rail and river transportation and with a sizable population, Troy was able to draw on the best of traveling theater groups, lecturers, and musicians of all sorts. *Courtesy of Rensselaer County Historical Society*

In 1804 Phebe Warren, a member of St. Paul's Episcopal Church, began instructing young girls in the catechism. After the War of 1812, she conducted a local Saturday sewing school for the girls from poor neighborhoods until her death in 1835. Phebe's daughter-in-law, Mary Warren, then took over the school and extended her instruction to include reading, writing, and singing.

In 1844 Mary Warren built the Church of the Holy Cross, the first Episcopal church in the area to eliminate the pew charges which often kept poorer residents from becoming members. Holy Cross gained national notice by becoming the first church in America to use the choral service developed in English cathedrals. Girls from the Warren School performed the music, soon to be copied in hundreds of other churches.

The school continued well into the twentieth century before closing. The Institute, rectory, and church still stand today and are currently in the process of being rehabilitated. *Illustration from Weise,* City; *courtesy of Rensselaer County Historical Society*

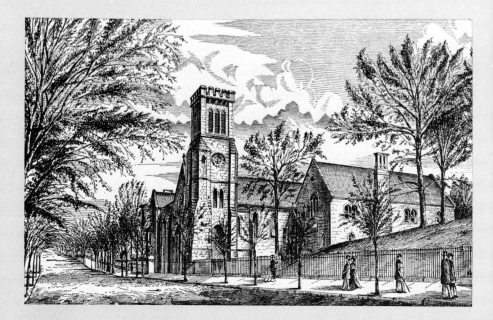

James C. Comstock, a Lansingburgh teacher and school principal, is to be credited with leading the way to truly public schools. Comstock was instrumental in the passage of an act in the state legislation which created a special local school district in Lansingburgh. This district was empowered to raise funds for operating expenses by real estate taxation, thus making a free school for children possible. One year later this district's system was used as a model for a statewide act extending the free school system throughout New York.

The Lansingburgh school was named after Comstock, although it was also known as the Market Street School. Built in 1845 on the northeast corner of 115th Street and Fifth Avenue, the school (shown here) stood until 1910 when a new high school was built on the site. *Henry A. Foy photo; courtesy of Frances D. Broderick*

Typical of the one-room schoolhouses which dot Rensselaer County is this one, built in the early 1800s in Stephentown. Over the years, as populations expanded and transportation improved, many district schools were consolidated. Those left empty by the moves were then closed or converted to other uses—such as a town hall or library—or into a private home like this structure which was District School No. 7, the Garfield School. *Courtesy of Stephentown Historical Society*

A classical school sponsored by the Methodists, Troy University was established in 1854, in brief competition with Rensselaer Polytechnic Institute. This imposing structure was built in 1858 and the college opened that fall with sixty students but only lasted until 1862. At the end of that year the buildings were sold to the Roman Catholic Church to become the Provincial Theological Seminary. It later became the Seminary for the Sisters of St. Joseph. Lightning struck two of the steeples in later years and the remaining two then were torn down. RPI purchased the buildings in the 1950s. The Folsom Library now occupies the site while the chapel connected with the seminary has been renovated as the computer center. *Courtesy of Rensselaer County Historical Society*

A private school, the Troy Academy was incorporated in 1834 with the express purpose of providing preparatory training for students who wished to enter Rensselaer Polytechnic Institute. The school was located at Seventh and State streets and included special and general courses as well as military drills. An advertisement of the late 1800s promised that students were prepared "for business, for college, and for scientific schools." The academy actually shared teachers with RPI and was successful for a number of years. It closed in 1917. Illustrated are the building and the students in 1902.
Courtesy of Rensselaer County Historical Society

The famous Transylvania Institute was located in Brainard, on what was then the main road between Albany and Boston. The Institute, in service from 1838 until nearly the end of the century, was representative of many academies founded around the county in the 1830s and 1840s. These provided additional education (the equivalent of high school) to "young ladies and gentlemen." The Transylvania Institute typically accepted both day students from the surrounding countryside and boarders from states along the eastern seaboard as well as from farther west and south. Students studied history, grammar, languages, mathematics, astronomy, physics and philosophy. The long success of the Institute is attributed to Miss Henrietta V. Hicks, a local woman who served as principal and owner for many years until her death in 1885. The buildings were torn down in 1905.
Courtesy of G. Steven Draper

52

Founded in Sand Lake (now Averill Park) in 1852 was Scram's Collegiate Institute, a boarding school for boys, which opened with thirty-six students. Designed to prepare young men for college, it lasted until 1875 when the founder died. Horatio Averill then converted the building into a hotel which burned in 1921. The Church of the Covenant now stands on that site. Another Sand Lake institution, the Brookside Institute, lasted only from 1862 to around 1865, but the original building still stands. Other private boarding schools were scattered throughout the county to train children of middle and high school age. The McChesney home in Brunswick, the Transylvania Institute in Brainard, and the Poestenkill Academy were only a few. *Courtesy of New York State Library Manuscripts and Special Collections*

By 1850, Troy was trying to cope with congestion along River Street, its commercial center, caused by three railroad lines which terminated there. In 1851, The Troy Union Railroad Company was formed to build and operate a new Union Station on property on Sixth Street, between Fulton Street and Broadway. The new station, complete with an enclosed train shed one block long, became a hub for passenger travel in and out of the growing city. Freight houses and large rail yards built in the northern and southern parts of the city became important centers of commercial activity. The Great Fire of 1862 destroyed the original station, but a new depot was immediately erected to serve the railroads connecting Troy with markets in all compass directions.

Here is a schedule of passenger trains arriving at and departing from Troy Union Station in 1864. Railroad employees were warned to be on the lookout at all times for freight trains, particularly ore trains to and from the Rensselaer, Burden, and Albany Iron Works in the southern part of the city.

The 1863 depot was replaced in 1902 and the new building torn down in 1958 but local telephone directories continued to list a number for the defunct Troy Union Railroad Company until 1986. *Courtesy of G. Steven Draper*

No. 11.
TROY UNION RAIL ROAD.
FOR EMPLOYEES ONLY.
UNION DEPOT.

DEPARTURES.	ARRIVALS.
A. M. Passenger Trains.	**A. M. Passenger Trains.**
5:20..N. York Exp. & Boston.	4:50..Troy and Boston.
6:45..Hudson River Express.	6:25..N. Y. Central Express.
7:30..Rens. and Saratoga.	6:45..New-York.
8:00..Troy and Boston.	9:30..N. Y. Central Express.
8:30..N. Y. Central Express.	10:00..Troy and Boston.
9:00..Albany and Boston Ex.	10:10..Albany.
9:15..Harlem.	10:15..Rens. and Saratoga.
9:45..Rens. and Saratoga.	
10:30..Hudson River Express.	**P. M.**
11:00..Albany and Poughkeep-	12:10..Albany and Springfield.
sie.	12:55..Hudson River Express.
P. M.	3:50..Troy and Boston Expr.
12:40..N. Y. Central Express.	4:15..N. Y. Central Express.
1:00..Troy & Boston Express.	4:15..Rens. and Saratoga.
3:00..Harlem Express.	4:55..Harlem.
3:45..Albany and Boston Ex.	5:15..Albany and Boston.
4:00..Hudson River Express.	5:40..Hudson River.
4:30..Troy and Boston.	7:45..N. Y. Central Express.
5:00..N. Y. Central Express.	7:55..Rens. and Saratoga.
5:00..Rens. and Saratoga.	8:32..Troy and Boston.
9:45..Troy and Boston.	9:40..Hudson River Express.
10:00..New-York.	10:25..Harlem Express.
12:10..N. Y. Central.	12:00..Hudson River Express.

Troy, Dec. 19, 1864.

ook out for **Freight Trains** at all times

Father Peter Havermans, a Catholic priest and one of Troy's greatest community leaders, was responsible for establishing many of the Catholic parochial schools of the county. Because Catholics tended to concentrate in urban areas, Troy had most of the parochial schools with others in Rensselaer and Hoosick.

In 1845 Father Havermans founded St. Mary's parish in Troy as well as St. Mary's School. He served the Catholic Church for fifty-five years and established several elementary and six secondary schools in the course of those years. He was also responsible for the founding of the first Troy Hospital (now St. Mary's), whose cornerstone was laid on Washington and Hill streets in 1849. *Illustration from Sylvester, History; courtesy of Rensselaer County Historical Society*

Winter's arrival was greeted with joy in the days before a bridge was built across the Hudson River at Albany. The frozen river heralded the beginning of a gala social season, opening up that barrier to traffic from both sides of the river. One popular crossing point was at the ferry landing in Bath-on-Hudson (later part of Rensselaer). The Boston and Albany Railroad ended at this point and all of its freight was ferried across the river to Albany a little north of Maiden Lane while passengers could go either there or to the foot of State Street. The baggage sled has just been loaded in this 1854 engraving, and the driver is preparing to follow the sleds carrying passengers. Others crossed the river in small sleds or on foot. A bridge did not span the river in this section until a railroad bridge was built in 1866. A bridge for teams and carriages did not open for sixteen more years.

Built in 1841 as the Eastern Railroad, the Boston and Albany Railroad was once the longest and most expensive railroad constructed by a single corporation. It climbed out of the Hudson Valley toward Chatham and continued eastward to Boston through

Shown here is the interior of the W. A.
Sherman store at 259 River Street, Troy.
Magill photo; courtesy of Troy Public Library

Chapter Four

1861-1899
The Full Bloom Of Industry

As the Civil War loomed on the horizon, county residents were active in supporting the abolitionist movement. Henry Highland Garnet, an ex-slave who came to Troy to become minister of the Liberty Street Presbyterian Church, published a well-known national abolitionist weekly, *The Clarion,* from his church office. Another powerful anti-slavery piece, *Uncle Tom's Cabin,* by Harriet Beecher Stowe, was first produced as a play on stage at the Troy Museum in 1852. It ran for 150 consecutive nights.

When words became actions, the thirty miles of Hudson riverfront provided ample cover for sections of an Underground Railroad for escaped slaves fleeing to Canada. Once war broke out, Rensselaer County citizens rallied to support the cause. The Second Regiment of New York State Volunteers, organized in the spring of 1861 with nine hundred soldiers from the county and surrounding areas, was the first volunteer unit to serve in Virginia. Many other local men went off to fight in the war, often contributing their lives to the cause. The county's industries, crucial in providing goods for the Union army, expanded their production to meet the needs. In addition to the well-known Troy industries that produced such indispensible items as horseshoes, ammunition, and the *Monitor,* were county factories such as the Powder Works in Valley Falls.

The decades after the Civil War found the industries in Rensselaer County continuing to prosper, with many of the companies reaching their height of production in the last quarter of the century. Walter A. Wood, Henry Burden, and the Gurley Company gained international recognition for their inventions. The collar and shirt industry, begun in Troy and spread throughout the county, came to produce over 90 percent of America's detachable collars and many of its finest shirts.

Although agricultural production continued to rise

due to increased mechanization and improved plants, the actual number of farms began to decline by 1879 as over-used fields wore out and workers moved to the better paying jobs of the city. In many small towns, farmers and their wives supplemented their income by taking in piecework from local factories, principally from shirt factories.

Immigrants brought their own customs and organizations into the various towns. As the middle class increased with prosperous times, more leisure time and money became available and recreational pursuits began to expand. A great fire devastated downtown Troy in 1862 but the city rebounded with vigor, replacing the seventy-five acres of charred rubble in just six months with a new Victorian city, bristling with telegraph lines and grand public buildings. In the last few years of the century, the villages of Bath-on-Hudson, East Albany, and Greenbush were incorporated into the county's second official city, Rensselaer. The county was ready to face another century.

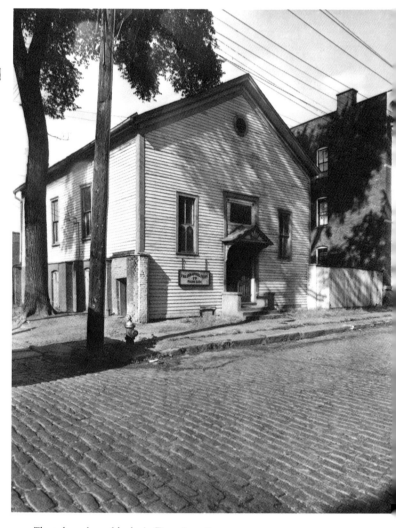

There have been blacks in Troy since its founding in 1789. Only fifteen years later, the city's population of 3,200 included eighty free blacks and seventy-nine slaves. By 1827 slavery was outlawed throughout the state.

Liberty Street Presbyterian Church, between Third and Fourth streets, was an early black church in Troy. Henry Highland Garnet was the pastor from 1843 to 1848. Born into slavery and educated at the famous Oneida Institute, Garnet gained national recognition after delivering a discourse against slavery to the House of Representatives in 1865. Members of Garnet's congregation were equally active. George Baltimore was instrumental in the organization of the first Negro State Convention, held in Troy in 1841. Out of that convention grew the forerunner of the NAACP. Liberty Street Presbyterian Church remained active for many years but the building no longer stands. Other active black congregations in the area were the Bethel Free Congregation, formed in 1832, and the Congregational Free Church, founded in 1842. *Courtesy of Rensselaer County Historical Society*

The Schaghticoke Woolen Mill was built in 1864, employing 175 people to manufacture "fancy cashmeres" on the most modern machinery available. The mill was powered by the Great Falls of the Hoosic River, which drop nearly one hundred feet in one half mile before the river empties into the Hudson. An 1897 article in *The Troy Daily Times* described the company as "one of the foremost woolen manufacturers in the country." At that time the mighty machinery of the plant processed about 145,000 pounds of Australian wool each month. The wool was first washed in a machine 130 feet in length, then burred, and carefully dyed. The precisely dyed wool was conveyed by an early form of automation to specific rooms on the fourth floor for blending. The wool was carded, spun, dressed, and then woven into cloth, which required fulling, shearing, and pressing before it was finally measured on automatic machinery, and sold to fine tailors and manufacturers.

Schaghticoke Woolen Mill went through six owners and several business failures in its forty-four years of operation. After sale of its machinery and nearly a quarter of a century of idleness, the great complex was demolished in 1932. *Courtesy of Rensselaer County Historical Society*

The Civil War had a devastating effect on the lives of Rensselaer County citizens. Throughout the county, hundreds of young men volunteered to fight for the Union cause. For many it was their first trip outside the state, and a great number of them did not return from the battlefields. Monuments to those who died can be found in almost every town.

In Lansingburgh, a photographer recorded the departure from Young's Grove of a proud company of young men at the beginning of the war, and he then gathered the remnants of that same company around 1870 for a reunion photograph. Only half of the original number remained. The harsh effects of war can be seen in the lost limbs and general aging of this once virile group. *James Irving photo; courtesy of Warren F. Broderick*

Maj. Gen. John Ellis Wool, one of Troy's most distinguished soldiers, died in Troy in 1869 at the age of eighty-six. Many generals, military units, and the governor of New York attended his funeral, while thousands watched his funeral procession from St. Paul's Church to Oakwood Cemetery.

Wool had a remarkable military career, serving first in the War of 1812, then as second in command to Zachary Taylor during the Mexican War. For his gallantry in Mexico, General Wool was awarded three ornate swords in elaborate ceremonies by the Congress of the United States, the New York State Legislature, and his home city of Troy. Wool came out of retirement at the age of seventy-five to assist in the Civil War. He was promoted to major general and appointed commander of the Department of the East before retiring again in 1863.

Wool left fifty thousand dollars in his will to be used to erect a monument on his grave-site. Much engineering ingenuity was required to move the sixty feet high, one hundred ton granite monolith from Vinal Haven, Maine, to Oakwood Cemetery. After traveling by boat to Troy, it was moved on rollers to a prominent site three hundred feet above the Hudson River. It was supported by an elaborate scaffold and carefully raised by ropes and pulleys. The base of the monument bears an inscription composed by William Cullen Bryant. *Courtesy of Rensselaer County Historical Society*

The Great Fire of 1862 began on May 10, when sparks from a locomotive set ablaze the covered bridge of Rensselaer and Saratoga Railroad (now the location of the Green Island bridge). A northwest gale spread the flames quickly that Saturday starting shortly after the noon hour. Although firemen from as far as Albany fought the giant fire, by evening it had claimed five lives, including that of a blind man, and 507 buildings, not including barns and outhouses. It devastated seventy-five acres of Troy's downtown from Federal Street to Congress Street, and from River Street as far as Eighth Street and part of Ninth Street. In this photo taken soon thereafter, the man with a horse and wagon is on Fifth Avenue, facing the corner of Fulton Street. At the top of the photo is the Warren residence, "Mt. Airy," and Troy University which became St. Joseph's Provincial Seminary in 1864. The round-topped wall at right is part of the shell of the Troy Union Station. Several churches, banks, Rensselaer Polytechnic Institute's building at State Street and Sixth Avenue, hundreds of stores and many dwellings all went up in flames. The damage added up to $2,677,892 of which $1,321,874 was covered by insurance. Contributions from a wide area totaled more than fifty thousand dollars. Reconstruction began immediately and by November of the same year all of the central city had been completely rebuilt. *Courtesy of Joseph A. Parker*

JOSEPH FOX, LANSINGBURG, N. Y.

As steam-powered machinery emerged as a more rapid means of manufacturing, the Fox Company adopted it to become a major producer of crackers in the Lansingburgh area. Joseph Fox patented a cracker machine in 1860 which contributed greatly to his success. The plant became known as the Fox Steam Cracker Company; it was located at 116th Street and Second Avenue, on the site of the present Marine Midland Bank. *Courtesy of Lansingburgh Historical Society*

In 1867 James Irving photographed the laying of the cornerstone for Troy's new First Ward School at River and Liberty streets. The First Ward encompassed the area between Liberty and Congress streets from the River on the west to Seventh Avenue on the east. The earlier school was on Fifth Avenue below Ferry Street. The school was built of Croton brick with Ohio sandstone embellishments, and an interior of polished and oiled chestnut wood. It opened in 1869 with three departments: the grammar, the intermediate, and the primary departments. The building was designed by Marcus Fayette Cummings, who moved to Troy after the fire of 1862 and became the primary architect in rebuilding Troy. For the rest of the century, he and his son Frederick continued to design churches, homes, businesses, and public buildings that give Troy a grace and dignity befitting its position as the seat of county government. It is quite possible that Cummings himself is among the party pictured here. *Courtesy of Rensselaer County Historical Society*

These charcoal sheds in Mattison Hollow, South Berlin, were part of a large-scale commercial venture, just one of numerous charcoal pits operating in the southeastern towns of Rensselaer County from the early 1800s well into this century. The Berlin operation utilized a small two-car inclined railway to carry wood from mountain forests to the kiln which can be seen in the background of this photograph from around the turn of the century. The full car at the top of the hill came down by gravity, pulling on the empty car at the bottom and sending it up for the next load. Atop the kiln is Mike Collins, who was in charge of burning.

The airless burn required to make charcoal was achieved by closely stacking wood in stone or brick kilns, or in earth-covered "pits" with a central chimney. The fire had to be closely watched so that the wood smoldered rather than burst into flame. There are still many residents of the charcoal-making towns who once had their own operations or who remember the smoke rising from the coal pits

in the mountains and the sound of high-racked coal wagons rumbling through town before daybreak with their city-destined loads. Although charcoal had domestic uses, it was more importantly the fuel used in the iron furnaces of Troy and Albany, the glass furnaces of Sand Lake, and other industries where a high controlled temperature was needed. *J. F. Cowee photo; courtesy of Rensselaer County Historical Society; illustration from Benjamin and Park,* Cyclopaedia

The blacksmith shop was an important center in every town and hamlet. The smith performed many necessary services, from shoeing horses, mules, and oxen to repairing iron machine parts, as well as making wagon tires, tools, and decorative ironware. Photographer James E. West recorded Nathan L. Hakes at work on his anvil in 1899. *Courtesy of New York State Library Manuscripts and Special Collections*

Across the mill pond in the Brunswick hamlet of Eagle Mills (then called Millville) can be seen a sawmill, general store, hotel and carriage house, and foundry. A drop of twenty-five feet at this point of the Poestenkill powered numerous mills and shops from the late eighteenth through the nineteenth centuries. Down the road past the carriage is the four-story Eagle Flouring Mill, built in the 1820s, and later occupied by Planters

Hoe Company.

Another center of water-powered industry in Brunswick was in Cropseyville on the Quackenkill. A gristmill there shipped sixty-two thousand bushels of corn, rye flour, oats, and buckwheat to New York City in 1890. Such mills were small but important links in Rensselaer County's chain of agriculture, industry, and commerce. *Courtesy of Brunswick Town Historian*

Established in 1888, Ingalls' Oak Grove Paper Mills was one of three paper mills in Castleton-on-Hudson at the turn of the century. The largest of these, originally owned by Charles Van Benthuysen, was Woolworth and Graham Fort Orange Paper Company. At one time this company employed two hundred people, and produced two million postal cards per day for the United States government. *Courtesy of Castleton-on-Hudson Village Archives*

The history of paper making in Rensselaer County probably started at Mahlon Taylor's mill on the lower Poestenkill Gorge before 1792. By 1846 Manning, Howland and Williams were operating a paper mill in the upper gorge which made paper from recycled hemp rope. The factory, later Manning Paper Company, was said to be the largest manufacturer of rope manila paper in the world. Manning operated a mill at that site until 1962, the most enduring of a long list of industries that used the water power of Benjamin Marshall's Mount Ida complex in the Poestenkill Gorge. The Manning Paper Company still produces high-quality papers in their plant in Green Island. *Courtesy of John Peckham*

Ruff's Grist Mill (pictured here around 1890) is one of many substantial industries built on the Lower Poestenkill from the Hudson River up into Poestenkill Gorge. The first recorded mill on the Poestenkill was on or very near this site. Ruff's Mill was established by Andrew Ruff in 1871 and was active until 1929. The last of his mill buildings, a tall brick structure, burned in 1968.

The stream's hundred-foot drop at the upper end of the Poestenkill Gorge created power for a major nineteenth-century industrial complex. Benjamin Marshall fully utilized this resource when he built a dam in 1840 and carved a raceway, six hundred feet in length, through the rock wall of the gorge. The water rushed through that tunnel to activate turbines in his cotton factory and provide energy for numerous other mills as it dropped down to the Hudson River. The gorge was lined with densely packed mills producing paper, wire, cotton material, lumber, and more for over a hundred years. Flooding caused by the hurricane of 1938 destroyed all of the structures along the north bank. Today the site shows few signs of its industrial past and a park has been developed to preserve the area and its past. *Magill photo; courtesy of Troy Public Library*

The Eagle Brewery was established in 1865 by Samuel Bolton on the west side of Second Avenue. It was one of the largest industries in Lansingburgh and specialized in ale and porter. Many other breweries existed in the urban areas. In 1886 ten breweries in Troy brewed ale, porter, and lager beer; brewing was a major industry up until the twentieth century. Fitzgerald Brothers was the last of the breweries to remain, going out of business in 1962. *Courtesy of Frances D. Broderick*

Castleton-on-Hudson in 1890 was a village two blocks wide, little different from today. Docks jutted out into the water, and the Hudson River Railroad passed by at the water's edge. Castleton's thriving shipping industry moved fortunes in hay, ice, paper, bricks, and other locally produced goods to New York City markets until it was supplanted by railroads and trucks. *Courtesy of Castleton-on-Hudson Village Archives*

Many a local farmer recalls ice-cutting as a winter job that allowed him to earn some cash and fill his own family ice house. Ice was cut from ponds and lakes as well as the Hudson River and either kept for personal use or sold to larger ice businesses. All of the harvesting was done by hand through the end of the century, as these men are doing on Blake's Pond in Hoosick about 1900. The advent of electric refrigerators made the ice industry superfluous, and the ponds are left uncut today. *Courtesy of Hoosick Town Historian*

Castleton men cut prodigious amounts of ice from the frozen Hudson River, moving the huge blocks on conveyors to cavernous ice houses where the ice was stacked in layers with sawdust or straw for insulation. The ice was shipped to New York and points beyond throughout the course of the year. A turn-of-the-century account notes that the ice business employed "one hundred in summer and ten times that in winter," when they harvested five to eight hundred tons of ice. Rensselaer County ice, cut on the Hudson River from Schaghticoke to Schodack and harvested from ponds in every town, was sold as far away as India, and as close as city rowhouses. *Courtesy of Castleton-on-Hudson Village Archives*

The Johnsonville Axe Manufacturing Company operated beside the Hoosic River from 1859 to 1906, one of the many industries which used the river and the railroad to good advantage in this Pittstown hamlet. The factory was later owned by the American Edge Tool Company, then by Lane, Gale and Company. It turned out hundreds of thousands of axes annually, sending them to all parts of the world. The large building also housed a gristmill, as the sign indicates. *Courtesy of Pittstown Historical Society*

Cable Flax Mills had its origins in Waterford, where it operated for fifty-six years, enduring several owner and name changes before moving to Troy in 1868. Three years later the company moved to Schaghticoke and merged with Schaghticoke Linen Mill (in business since 1810). By the 1880s Cable Flax Mills was producing hemp and linen twine around the clock, and the plant had doubled in size. It was not unusual in the nineteenth century to have young children working in the mills in the less skilled jobs. Many of the men and boys in this circa 1890 photograph have descendents still living in Schaghticoke today.

Business at the mill expanded with large orders from the government during the First World War, and the number of employees swelled to well over 250. After the war, however, demand lessened as bags and gummed tape replaced the need for twine, and operations slumped, ceasing altogether in 1929. The huge mill buildings were then demolished. *Courtesy of Richard Lohnes*

James K. P. Pine was a native of Hoosick who began business in Troy in the 1860s and eventually became president of Lansingburgh's largest industry, the United Shirt and Collar Company. The company was a consolidation (1890) of Pine's company and four other well-established plants. Together they were one of this country's foremost manufacturers of shirts and collars. Pine was also president of the People's Bank of Lansingburgh (1888), founder and president of The Troy Record Company, one of the founders of Samaritan Hospital (both 1896), and trustee of the Troy Savings Bank (1892). The illustration advertises one of the many products made in United's mammoth plant at Second Avenue and 120th Street. Also known as the Lion Shirt factory, the building covered an entire block and was one of the largest mill buildings in the area when it was built. The building still stands today and is occupied by Standard Manufacturing. *Courtesy of Warren F. Broderick*

Although the detachable collar and shirt industries were funded and based in Troy, large portions of the business were farmed out to smaller factories and home workshops around the county. The shirt factory shown here was in operation above the Petersburg Post Office around the turn of the century. Frank Reynolds had a shirt factory over his Petersburg store in 1870, but moved the factory to his gristmill fifteen years later when the store burned down. Reynolds employed twenty-five people in his factory in 1897. That same year, another Petersburg shirt factory—Kellyer, Reynolds and Sweet—reported having little help in the factory, but as many as four hundred people who worked at home. Operations such as these could be found in dozens of Rensselaer County towns. *Courtesy of Judy Rowe*

The Huyck Mill started in Rensselaerville in Albany County in 1870 and moved to Rensselaer in 1894. For many years blankets were Huyck's primary product. Some time after they moved to Rensselaer, they were reported to be the largest woolen mill in the country. They eventually diversified their production and began making papermakers' felts, which are used for forming and carrying paper products through rollers at paper mills. This picture of part of the Huyck work force was taken outside the mill about 1920.

In 1973 F. C. Huyck moved its corporate offices south and they have now merged with another firm. The Rensselaer plant closed in the 1980s and is being converted to offices and condominium apartments. *Fred S. Bullent collection; courtesy of Alice Lawrence*

Troy was the stove center of the United States in the mid-1800s, having at one time more than two hundred stove manufacturers. The Fuller and Warren Company was Troy's largest and longest-lived stove factory. These Fuller and Warren employees are shown about 1913 in the casting room. In the foreground a mold for a stove door can be seen. *Courtesy of the Times Record*

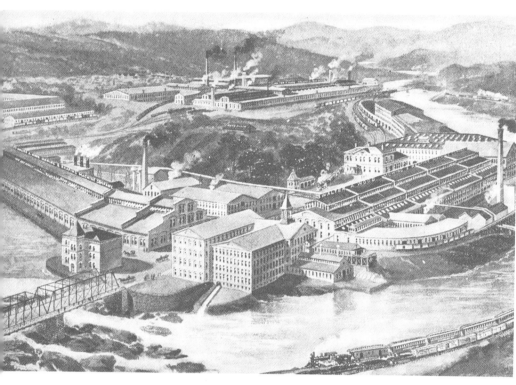

For much of the nineteenth century the Walter A. Wood Mowing and Reaping Machine Company managed to anticipate farmers' needs from Rensselaer County to Russia with each new product. By 1890 the company was the keystone of Hoosick Falls' vigorous economy, covering eighty-five acres of land beside the Hoosic River. There were seven miles of railroad track between the plant and the local tracks of the Fitchburg line on which two locomotives with freight cars ran, moving raw materials in and finished products out. Private electric and steam plants, the latter fueled by sawdust from the woodworking shops, provided light and heat for the two thousand employees. Undoubtedly inspired by two disastrous fires in earlier buildings, the plant had its own water tower, complete sprinkler system, and fire apparatus. In the exuberant spirit of the time, there was even a Walter A. Wood band.

Wood died in 1892, at a time when powerful farm machinery manufacturers were thriving in the Midwest. Steam and gasoline-powered farm machinery was first made available to farmers in the early twentieth century, but the Wood Company continued to produce only horse-drawn equipment. Because of their inability to respond to a changing world, the great works closed in 1924. Pictured is a panoramic view of the Wood complex from an 1894 catalog, as well as an interior view of the mower packing room.
Courtesy of Hoosick Town Historian; William P. Clark photo; courtesy of Lawrence Torpey

Nineteenth-century farmers were able to vastly improve their productivity with an ever-expanding variety of machines. In 1895 James E. West photographed the Thomas family in Petersburg, proudly posing with their most valuable farm possessions: a good pair of oxen and a mower which was undoubtably one of Wood's best selling models. Pictured are (left to right) Lewis Thomas, his son Hiram, Darius Thomas, and Lottie (Mrs. Warren) Thomas. Their farm was on the road from Babcock Lake Road to Stillman's Village. Although Wood shipped farming machinery all over the world, many of his best customers were farming families like the Thomases. *Courtesy of New York State Library Manuscript and Special Collections*

As local industries expanded and prospered, they created a newly wealthy middle class. This prosperity was expressed in a variety of new architectural styles. The vertical board-and-battens of Mrs. George Gould's Gothic-style country house "Oaklands" could be seen in similar houses in other parts of the county, all built in the mid-nineteenth century. The veranda across the front of the house was an important feature frequently used by the family for sitting, talking, and entertaining as the many plants and elaborate furniture suggest. Many houses which lacked a porch had one added in this same period.

George Gould was a wealthy Troy lawyer who served as city mayor in 1852 and later became a Justice of the State Supreme Court. *Courtesy of Rensselaer County Historical Society*

The thriving industries of the 1800s, which brought great wealth to their owners, created other forms of work as well. The new men of wealth built palatial mansions on large estates throughout the county and hired dozens of local people as servants, cooks, and maids. The rise of interest in gardening by mid-century led to the employment of an outdoor staff to maintain extensive lawns, elaborately patterned flowerbeds and carefully groomed shrubs. Walter A. Woods' private estate in Hoosick Falls required at least fifteen gardeners to keep up the grounds and greenhouses. They took a brief break from their work to pose with their tools for the photographer in 1887. *Courtesy of Lawrence Torpey*

The D. A. Judson and Company Coal Dealers, located along the river at Lansingburgh, were among twenty-nine coal dealers listed in the 1901 county directory. The Delaware and Hudson Canal, completed in 1829, linked the Hudson River at Roundout with the great anthracite coal fields in northeastern Pennsylvania. By the 1870s the railroads were bringing in most of the coal used by the county's growing population and industries for heating, iron smelting, and steam generation. The D. A. Judson and Company office, located on First Avenue above 118th Street, no longer stands. *Van Schoonhoven photo; courtesy of Frances D. Broderick*

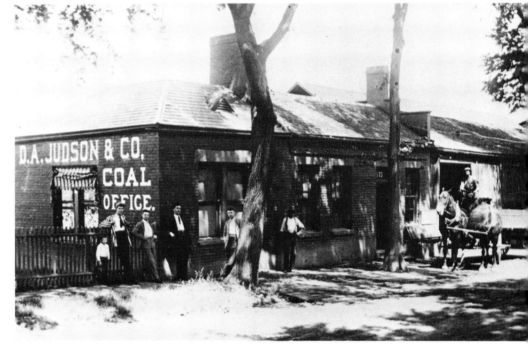

The Gasholder House in Troy is one of the few remaining examples of a building type once common in most northeastern cities. The Troy Gas Light Company, which first supplied the city with illuminating gas in 1848, built it in 1873 at the corner of Jefferson Street and Fifth Avenue. Frederick Sabatton, a well known gas works engineer, designed the building. His father, Paul Sabatton, was a close friend of Robert Fulton and prepared plans and specifications for the *North River Steamboat,* later known as the *Clermont.* The masonry gasholder contained a large telescoping iron tank which sat like an inverted cup in a pool of water twenty-two feet below ground level. The tank went up and down to maintain a constant pressure in the pipes from the gasholder to homes, businesses, and street lamps across the city.

Gasholder buildings were enclosed to protect this iron tank from ice, snow, and high winds. The enclosure also prevented water from freezing in the holder pit, while its ornamental brick exterior projected an impressive corporate image. A unique feature of the building is its delicate radial truss roof structure (with no interior support), which is topped by a metal cupola with windows, once used for ventilation.

The building was taken out of service in the 1920s when a new central plant was built in Menands. The metal tank was removed in 1930, and the pit filled in. In subsequent years, Oscar C. Buck, a circus manager, used the huge building to store equipment, and local bands used it for marching practice. The current owner, a painting contractor, uses it for storage. A drawing of the building has become the symbol of the nationwide Society for Industrial Archeology. *Courtesy of Rensselaer County Historical Society*

When coming into Troy from the eastern part of the county to shop, you could leave horse and wagon at one of the many livery stables on Congress Street and find any kind of merchandise within a few blocks. Hull's Hardware was one of those shops that had a great variety as seen in this photo from around 1890. Judging from the number of childrens' sleds and sleighs on display, winter must be just around the corner. These sleds changed little in design from the time of the early Dutch settlers. *Magill photo; courtesy of Troy Public Library*

G. V. S. Quackenbush, at Broadway and Third streets, was one of Troy's best known emporiums. Gerrit Van Schaick Quackenbush first opened dry goods stores at Franklin Square and then at 202 River Street. Soon after he built this splendid building, the panic of 1857 occurred, but Quackenbush had weathered the earlier depression of 1839-1840, and he survived this one as well. He is reported to have paid larger salaries than any other merchant, and was renowned as one of the founders of Troy's prosperity. His family carried on the business after his death. In 1937 Quackenbush's was one of the casualties of the Great Depression. W. T. Grant occupied the building until 1975, and Rite Aid Pharmacy is the present tenant. *Courtesy of Rensselaer County Historical Society*

The Troy Savings Bank was incorporated in 1823, just thirteen years after a Scottish parson pioneered the idea of savings banks to encourage thrift among the working class. The bank initially was open on Saturday evenings and served depositors from towns throughout Rensselaer County, as well as those from Troy stores and factories. The first depositor was a black woman, Martha Jefferson, who deposited twenty dollars on the evening of August 30, 1823. The bank thrived, and in 1845 it built and moved into the Athenaeum (subsequently owned by the Troy YMCA), a stately Greek Revival style building at 10 First Street in the section known as "Banker's Row."

By 1871 the bank's trustees had chosen George B. Post's plans from among those submitted by five different architects for their present building at Second and State streets. A list of Troy Savings Bank's early trustees reads like a list of Troy's leading citizens, among them Hart, Warren, Vail, Marshall, Griswold, Burden, Winslow, Fuller, Gurley, Manning, Cluett, and Pine.

On April 19, 1875, Troy Savings Bank opened the Music Hall, located in the upper floors of their new building, with a "Grand Inauguration Concert." Today, as it has been for more than a century, fine music is regularly performed in that great hall, a concert space world-renowned for its superb acoustics. *Courtesy of Rensselaer County Historical Society*

Toward the end of the nineteenth century the rising middle class in the towns, villages, and cities tried to copy the life style of the rich. They decorated the exteriors of their homes with fancy woodwork, added porches, turrets, and towers, and filled their homes with large pieces of furniture, frequently of oriental influence, as evidence of their prosperity. It was a time when families also ordered a piano or parlor organ. There was a great demand for piano teachers and young ladies often captivated potential suitors with a display of their talent at the keyboard. E. H. Miller's piano showroom was one of many places in the county where pianos and organs could be bought. Another firm, Cluett and Sons, started in Troy in 1854 and sold instruments by major makers such as Steinway and Chickering. It had outlets throughout the Capital District, western Vermont and Massachusetts. *Magill photo; courtesy of Troy Public Library*

Troy was a commercial center well before its factories drew national attention. A large variety of shops existed and businessmen were attracted to the area from its earliest days. "This country is the best for business I ever saw...done more business in one day than in one week in Providence," wrote Benjamin Covell to his brother Silas back home in 1789. More than a century later downtown Troy was in an age of transition when the jungle of overhead wires said "Progress!", while horses vied with trolleys for the right-of-way. At the right is the old Fulton Market, a classic, columned building on River Street at the foot of Fulton Street. Every day scores of wagons converged on Troy, like the delivery from Brunswick Creamery, to furnish the tons of hay, ice, wood and charcoal, meat and produce, and other agricultural products that kept Troy humming. After making their deliveries or purchases, the visitors may have dropped in on the Lucas Confectionary on Second Street for the ice cream known throughout the county for its quality. Although this market district has changed over the years, many of the buildings remain. *Courtesy of Rensselaer County Historical Society*

The corner entrance is still a distinctive feature at 156 Broadway, Rensselaer, where W. P. Irwin built this structure and founded the East Albany Banking and Trust Company in 1873. Irwin owned a number of factories in the area: one malt house was at the river's edge, another malt house lay on Mill Creek just below the Irwin flour mill. Still farther up the creek Irwin laid out a vast ornate complex which included several houses, extensive drives, parks, a summer house, bowling alley, "grapery," and other structures. *Illustration from Beers,* Atlas; *courtesy of Rensselaer County Historical Society*

Troy's government dates back to 1791. The town's first formal offices were in the 1831 Rensselaer County Court House and later in the 1845 Athenaeum Building at 10 First Street. As the city grew in size and wealth, Mayor Edward Murphy's administration authorized the construction of a city hall in 1875 at the southeast corner of State and Third streets, the site of the Third Street burial ground. (The bodies were reinterred in Oakwood and Mount Ida cemeteries). A new three-story brick building was designed by Marcus Cummings and completed in October 1876. The hall's tower contained a large clock and a 66,000-pound fire alarm bell. The City Hall served Troy well for sixty-two years until October 28, 1938 when a night fire roared through the structure. After the fire, it was determined that the building was beyond repair and the remaining brick exterior was torn down. The major city offices moved to the second floor of the Central Fire Station at 51 State Street. For many years it was felt that the city could not afford a new municipal building, and a new city hall did not open its doors to local residents until 1974. *Courtesy of Rensselaer County Historical Society*

In the summer of 1886 the federal government bought three buildings at the corner of Fourth Street and Broadway for $99,891. The site was for a new post office for Troy. It cost about $400,000 to build the imposing three-story stone structure which had a 160-foot high square tower and numerous fireplaces. Completed in 1891, the post office also provided offices for the Department of Good Roads and the Internal Revenue Service. The third floor was used as a stamp distribution center for area post offices. In the 1930s, when the old building became inefficient for the increased flow of mail, a community debate ensued over whether to expand the fort-like structure or build a new one. Because of the Depression, the Post Office Department favored a new building to create jobs. As a result, the massive building was torn down in 1936, just a year after this photo was taken. *Courtesy of Rensselaer County Historical Society*

In 1791 when Rensselaer County was separated from Albany County by act of the state legislature, a competition arose between Troy and Lansingburgh for the site of the new county courthouse. Troy won with a gift of land on the southeast corner of Second and Congress streets. Since then three buildings have occupied the site. The original brick structure was completed in 1794 with an adjacent small jail completed in 1795. As the population grew, this was replaced in 1831 with a marble structure in the Greek Revival style at a cost of forty thousand dollars. It provided sufficient space for Troy city officials and the Common Council until the first city hall was constructed in 1876. The third and present granite courthouse was designed by Troy architects Marcus Cummings and his son, Frederick. Constructed between 1894 and 1898 at a cost of $346,000, the interior is distinguished by marbleized columns, paneled oak, and bronze balustrades. In 1912 the Second Street Presbyterian Church adjacent to the courthouse was purchased to accommodate the expanding court needs. A connecting corridor, large courtroom, and new offices were constructed and the annex formally opened in 1915. *Courtesy of Rensselaer County Historical Society*

Originally drawn by the firemen, horse-drawn fire engines gave improved protection against the spread of fires. Volunteer fire companies were organized to protect different districts, often taking their name from the organizers or the largest sponsor. Troy's Arba Reed No. 1 Steamer Company was organized in 1860. The city later built a firehouse for the volunteer unit at State and Third streets. In 1922 the city changed to full-time paid firemen and the last of the horse-drawn vehicles were replaced by motorized vehicles two years later. As fire companies were further consolidated in the 1970s and 1980s, several of the remaining firehouses have been saved by adaptation to other uses. *Courtesy of Rensselaer County Historical Society*

Membership in a volunteer fire company was a matter of great pride, and much of a community's social life centered around the company. Firemen's parades in particular were colorful events for the entire community. In Castleton-on-Hudson the Citizen's (Volunteer) Engine Company posed in front of their first steamer engine at the old firehouse around the turn of the century. The flowers, gloves, and ribbons all suggest that another parade is in the offing. *Courtesy of Castleton-on-Hudson Village Archives*

The prosperity of Hoosick Falls, seen here at the turn of the century, was closely linked with the many industries that occupied the river banks near the falls. Early cotton mills gave way to the expanding Walter A. Woods factory, which was the town's most significant influence from 1852 to 1924. The tidy brick storefronts on John Street looking toward Main Street contain all the amenities expected from a town: Lurie's Leading Department Store, a bank, a hotel, a confectionary, and two ice cream parlors. Most of the buildings still stand, and a recent facade improvement program has restored many of the storefronts. *Courtesy of Hoosick Town Historian*

This Petersburg street scene, photographed in the late 1890s, shows Jones's store on the left, "the farmers' store," where merchandise was often sold by the hogshead, and catalogs at the counter offered every necessity from fencing to gravestones. Mr. Jones stocked plowshares and tractor parts, shoes and hats, food, notions, and even barbed wire. If it couldn't be found at Jones's Store, Erskine Sawyer might have it at his general store nearby. *James West photo; courtesy of New York State Library Manuscripts and Special Collections*

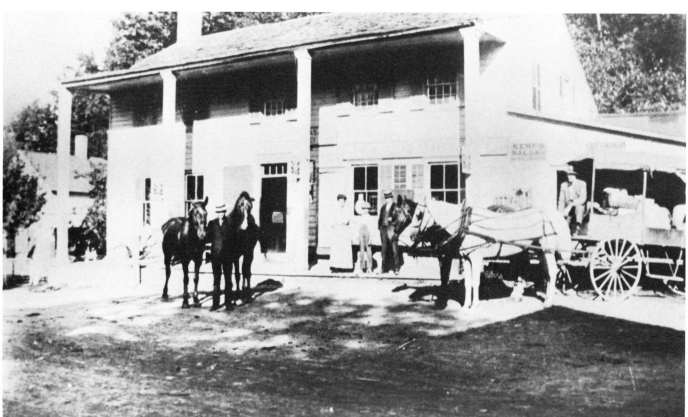

Known as the Pleasant Valley Store when this picture was taken around the turn of the century, this Cropseyville structure was built as one of the many inns for travelers on Brunswick's two major east-west roads. One of the town's first inns was Nathan Betts's in Center Brunswick, where citizens gathered for their first town meeting in 1807. Town records show that for many years innkeepers bid for the right to have the town meeting at their inn. Because they often had the largest space available, country inns throughout the county were used for lectures, church "donations," socials, and many other local gatherings. *Courtesy of Brunswick Historical Society*

Home deliveries of meat, bread, milk, and ice were made from wagons like this one photographed by Elmer Jacobs, although a two-horse team was not usual. The leather-thonged clothing and the hoods on the horses' ears are to keep the flies from annoying them. *Courtesy of Rensselaer County Historical Society*

This pastoral scene in Poestenkill in the early 1900s is typical, and it illustrates the virtual unanimity of "farmer" as an occupation. In an 1871 county gazetteer, the listing for one town begins with these occupations opposite the name: "teacher and farmer; blacksmith and farmer; sawmill and farmer; manufacturer of Star mowing machine and farmer; propri- etor of grist and saw mill and farmer; grocer and farmer; butcher and farmer; sawmill, lumber assessor and farmer; ex-school com- mitteeman and farmer. . . ." Farming was an integral part of life in Rensselaer County's villages, as well as on the more remote tracts of the towns. *Courtesy of Poestenkill Bicen- tennial Commission*

Delbert Eycleshymer was photographed tending sheep in Pittstown. *Courtesy of Pittstown Town Historian*

Sam Jones of Grafton, cutting hay, still actively farms in his seventies. *James West photo; courtesy of Judy Rowe*

M. J. Garrison photographed this fine team of oxen in East Schodack. Draft animals were necessary on the farm, and the slow, steady oxen were more powerful than horses. *Courtesy of Schodack Town Historian*

In 1890 Caroline Sherman Herrington had her picture taken feeding chickens on the Sherman farm in Pittstown. Many families kept chickens in the city as well. *Courtesy of Pittstown Town Historian*

Maple sugar is another locally-produced farm product which continues to be made today. The sap house on the Albert Mattison farm, circa 1900, was a good-sized establishment. The farm was located in Mattison Hollow in Cherry Plain, Berlin and had an average yield per year of more than a ton of maple sugar. *Courtesy of Berlin Historical Society*

The advent of the portable steam engine and the steam tractor changed the work methods of hundreds of people. Sawmills powered by a steam engine could be set up on the wood lot in locations far from dammed-up streams and waterfalls, and the steam tractor could haul loads easier than a team of horses. Old maps show many *SSM* on them, denoting "steam saw mill." On the farm, steam engines were used to power threshing equipment, as in this scene about 1890 on the Lynd farm in Poestenkill.

The Lynd farm, owned by the Wagners since 1952, continues to be worked by three Wagner sons and their families. They describe their operation as "mid-size," with 172 milking cows and 180 head of young stock. About four thousand bushels of potatoes are produced annually. Like many farmers, the Wagners have diversified. They now also board cattle scheduled for overseas shipment for the specified quarantine period, working in close compliance with federal Department of Agriculture regulations. *Courtesy of Poestenkill Historical Society*

One-room schools continued to be built throughout the nineteenth century in more rural areas. The Clove Road School in South Schodack was built in 1870 to replace an earlier building. Records tell the story of frugal local citizens who vetoed the purchase of additional land for a playground. They did, however, approve funds for buying coal to heat the building. The school was used until the end of World War II when it closed and the remaining children transferred to larger district schools. *Courtesy of Schodack Historical Society*

James Garfield, while a student at nearby Williams College, frequently visited the area. He taught lessons in penmanship and his name became connected with several local schools. The Moonlawn Road school in Eagle Mills was built in 1881, the year of Garfield's assassination, and is named after him. Used until the 1950s when a consolidated school was built, it is presently the headquarters of the Brunswick Historical Society. *Courtesy of Rensselaer County Historical Society*

First constructed as a two-room schoolhouse in 1886, the Castleton Union Free School on South Main Street grew over the years as its student population expanded. A second story and a tower with belfry were added within the first two years, and a rear wing with more classrooms was added in 1902. The architect for the original building, Frank J. Scott, also designed the elaborate Campbell and Scott mansions in the village of Castleton. The school no longer stands. *Courtesy of Rensselaer County Historical Society*

In 1895 the Troy Female Seminary changed its name to the Emma Willard School in honor of its founder. A statue was erected in front of the new Russell Sage Hall and alumnae of the school gathered around for a photographic record of the occasion.

The Emma Willard School continued to provide a strong secondary education for women from all over the United States. Many students married local men and stayed in the area, while others worked in towns across the country as teachers. One notable early graduate was Elizabeth Cady Stanton, a major force in the women's suffrage movement. *Courtesy of Rensselaer County Historical Society*

In June 1894, guests, workers, and a resident dog joined a group of Rensselaer Polytechnic Institute students in this photograph by one of the county's most famous photographers, James Irving, at Brown's Hotel, Crooked Lake. The surveying instruments are clues to a celebration ending a summer practice survey. The members of the Class of 1895 did a railroad survey and the Class of 1896 made a topographical and hydrological survey. Undoubtedly, the outcome of their work was used by the backers and builders of the Troy and New England Railway, started in 1895, to run from Albia to Averill Park. *Courtesy of Rensselaer Polytechnic Institute Archives*

By 1875 the boundaries of Rensselaer County townships had been defined in their current form. Poestenkill was separated from Sand Lake in 1848, while Greenbush was divided in 1855 into two sections: North Greenbush and Clinton. Within a few years, the latter had been renamed East Greenbush. Railroad lines ringed the edges of the county, connecting it with Bennington, Boston, and New York. Additional lines were proposed but never built through Sand Lake and the central townships. *Map from Beers,* Atlas; *courtesy of Rensselaer County Historical Society*

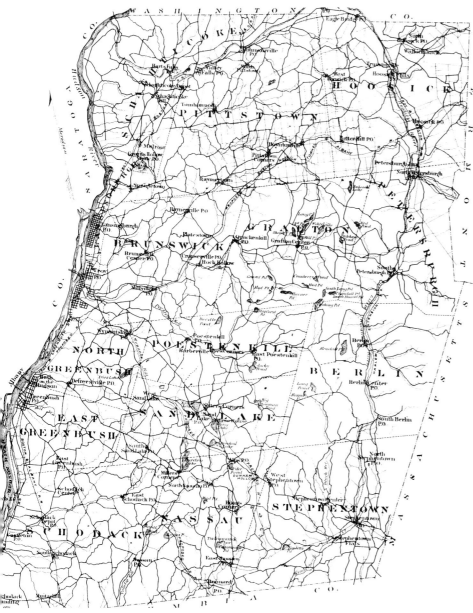

By far the most common type of bridge built in Rensselaer County between 1850 and 1925 was the metal truss bridge, which derived its structural form from the wooden covered bridges of the previous generations. Often prefabricated by specialized bridge companies, the truss bridges were strong, safe, and within the financial capabilities of the community in which they were built. Here is the Dublin Bridge at North Hoosick. *Thayer photo; courtesy of Rensselaer County Historical Society*

The Rutland Railroad's "Corkscrew Division" had its beginning in 1869, when Vermont interests constructed the line as a link from Bennington to Lebanon Springs, where a small line ran to Chatham and from there to New York City. The curved route following the Kinderhook Creek and Little Hoosic River provided rail service for the eastern half of the county but never could compete with the lines in the Hudson and Champlain valleys where speed was the rule. When the Rutland Railroad acquired the route in 1901, many of its milk trains went down the scenic valley through Petersburg, Berlin, Stephentown, and Brainard, but that was the only major business on the line.

Passenger service ended in 1931 and in an effort to survive, the Rutland abandoned the "Corkscrew Division" in 1953 and used other tracks through Troy and Rensselaer to get its trains to Chatham. Here the engineer and fireman of a small freight pause at the Stephentown station in 1953, the same year that the tracks were removed. The Vanderbilt House, built as a railroad hotel, is still in use but the station stands empty, its once painted boards weathered to a dark gray. *Jim Shaughnessy photo; courtesy of the photographer*

The Rutland Railway used the sand and gravel
hills along its right-of-way at Center Berlin as
sources of fill material for repairing washouts,
regular occurrences on the railroad. Here a
group poses on No. 477, looking as if they
had just conquered the steam-spewing
monster. The cuts these crews made into the
hillside can still be seen today from Route 22.
Courtesy of Katherine Wells

Johnsonville has played an intriguing role in Rensselaer County's railroad history. Both the Troy and Boston and the Albany Northern built lines through here in the 1850s. Competition proved too much for the Albany line which was abandoned in 1860. In 1870 the Greenwich and Johnsonville headed north from here across the Hoosic River to Washington County. Nine years later the Boston, Hoosac Tunnel and Western came through utilizing the roadbed of the abandoned earlier line. The area surrounding the depot included the Powers Hotel, the Fitchburg House, a freighthouse and turntable, all next to St. Monaca's Church.

In this early photograph the noon local from Troy had just arrived at the Johnsonville Station, and young boys parked their bikes to watch the flurry of activity surrounding the train before it departed. The last passenger train passed through Johnsonville in January 1958 and the tracks from here to Troy were removed in 1973. The G & J and its bridge are gone, as are the hotels. The depot still stands as a private residence, however, as does the Melrose Station farther along the abandoned roadbed. *R. A. Henry photo; courtesy of Jim Shaughnessy*

In the 1890s the "great ironhorse" was king, and the airplane and automobile had yet to be invented. No future means of transportation would achieve the personality of the old passenger train, nor the character and fascination of the passenger station. The hub of the small town or big city, the depot was the center of transportation, as well as the symbol of the high road to adventure and opportunity. Upon arriving at the Troy Depot, all of your transportation needs could be met by the Richards and Jordan Baggage Express Company. They specialized in cabs and carriages and had a large stable at 22-28 State Street. They advertised their availability for weddings and parties, as well as "special rates to theatrical companies." *Magill photo; courtesy of Troy Public Library*

Although now a suburban community for Troy, Melrose began as a farming town. For much of the nineteenth century, farm families took in summer boarders as city residents took advantage of the easy railroad access to escape the city. Trojans built large summer homes on Avenue "A" and Grand Boulevard with elaborate gardens, played quoits and croquet, and rode horses for enjoyment. Melrose also boasted of boarding houses and a hotel as seen from this business card. *Courtesy of Rensselaer County Historical Society*

Since the Civil War, baseball has been one of the most popular sports in Rensselaer County. Every town has had its own team and its traditional rivals. Particularly notable was the longstanding rivalry between villages on opposite sides of the Hudson River, as between the Castleton, Athens, and Catskill teams.

The most famous early local baseball team was the Lansingburgh Unions, called the "Haymakers," because they came from a small community and played teams from big cities. Founded in 1861, the Haymakers excelled between 1866 and 1869, when they won 90 percent of their games. Crowds of twenty-five hundred to five thousand fans attended the games played at four fields in Lansingburgh and North Troy. In 1869 they broke the Cincinnati Red Stockings winning streak with a nineteen-run tie game, played in Cincinnati and suspended by a near riot.

The Haymakers team lasted until 1872 when it disbanded. A subsequent Troy team of the same name became part of the first professional league called the National Association and 1879 entered the new National League. They remained in the National League until 1882, the last year of Troy's participation with national teams. *Courtesy of Warren F. Broderick*

Most high-wheel bicyclers were men like this group of Lansingburghians posing with their unwieldy steeds in 1884. The invention of safety bicycles with both wheels of equal size, brought thousands of men and women out onto the roads and into the countryside. By 1900, there were ten million safety bikes in the United States. The bicycle remained a popular mode of transportation until the 1920s when the automobile took over, but its recreational popularity has continued undiminished to the present day. *Courtesy of Rensselaer County Historical Society*

Although steam replaced wind as the source of power for vessels plying the Hudson River in the mid-century, the romance of sailing continued. Lansingburgh's generations of shipbuilders, sailors, and captains undoubtedly tested one another's abilities in friendly competitions on the river. *Courtesy of Frances D. Broderick*

GRAND REGATTA
AT LANSINGBURGH, N. Y.

Open to all Yachts not exceeding Forty Feet in length on the water line.

ENTRANCE FREE

Yachts will be divided in Three classes.

The 1st class consists of all boats 22 feet and upwards in length on the water line.

The 2nd class all boats 19 feet and up to 22 feet.

The 3rd class all boats under 19 feet.

THURSDAY, SEPT. 26, 1878.

Time allowance of thirty seconds to the foot according to the difference in length on the water line will be given to smaller yachts.

There will be two valuable prizes for each class to be awarded on the basis of time allowance.

So far as the same are applicable the race will be sailed according to the sailing regulations of the NEW YORK YACHT CLUB.

ENTRIES MAY BE MADE TO
J. H. KING, Lansingburgh, N. Y.
P. O. Box, 470.   On or before September 23rd.

Owner's measurement will be taken except in case of protest in which case the committee will measure the yacht. Instructions for sending the race, will be furnished on application any time after September 23rd.

Parties entering a Yacht will please furnish length of the vessel on the water line and captains of Yachts entered must report to the Regatta Committee before 12 A. M. of the day of the race.

Each Yacht will be be furnished with a designating number which must be carried throughout the race in a conspicuous place on the part side of the main sail

THE SEVERAL PRIZES WILL BE ANNOUNCED HEREAFTER.

Regatta Committee: CHAS. S. HOLMES.   W. N. MITER.   MARK L. FILLEY.
JOHN H. KING.   C. W. WITBECK

The brass band was a very democratic institution with players coming from all walks of life, unified through their performance of music. By the late nineteenth century, there were twenty-thousand bands in the United States. Every Rensselaer County town had one or more bands and most of them performed on special holidays and in the summertime at outdoor concerts, usually in the ubiquitous bandstands in the parks. This photo of the Berlin town band in 1888 shows a membership of youths and adults. Other well-known bands in the county were the Stephentown Band, Doring's Band, and Kirkpatrick's Band. Today the music programs of the various public and private schools produce many fine bands which march in local parades, play at celebrations and sports events, and often compete in nationally-known parades throughout the Eastern United States. *Courtesy of Rensselaer County Historical Society*

Organized in June 1866, the Laureate Boat Club had twelve members devoted to boating and rowing. Within a few years the club grew to include a boat house, a club house and an athletic field at the foot of Glen Avenue on the Hudson River in Troy. The club had as members famous oarsmen and individual athletes who held outstanding records in various fields. The club had football, baseball, and tennis teams and each year would present a show not unlike Harvard's Hasty Pudding. This photo shows the champion football team, Laureate 1896. Compared to the football equipment of today, one wonders how this team survived. As a club, it did not continue much after World War I. *Courtesy of Rensselaer County Historical Society*

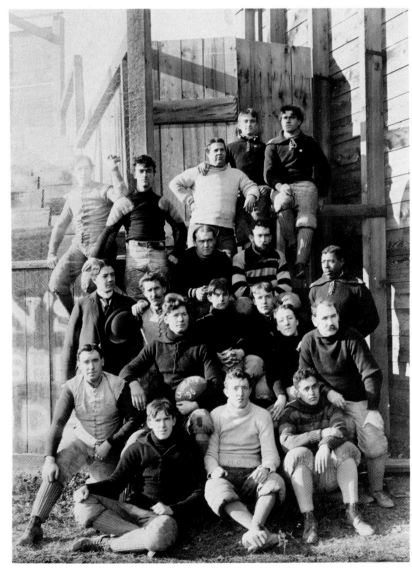

97

President William B. McKinley was in Troy on August 20, 1897 to attend a reunion of the Army of the Potomac. While here he was taken on a tour of the large Cluett, Coon and Company (later Cluett, Peabody and Company) plant on River Street. President McKinley is on the right side of the back seat. Sitting next to him is Troy's Mayor Francis J. Molloy. In the front seat facing the mayor is Arthur MacArthur, editor and publisher of the *Troy Northern Budget,* and facing the president is New York State Gov. Frank S. Black. Governor Black, a Trojan lawyer, was best known for completing the State Capitol in Albany, a project which had dragged on for thirty-two years. He commuted daily to Albany from his home which still stands on Pinewoods Avenue. *Courtesy of Rensselaer County Historical Society*

In 1892 the Rensselaer County Agriculture and Liberal Arts Society established a fair at Nassau. The fairgrounds were extensive and had many fine buildings for display in addition to a grandstand and racing oval. Annual activities included the wonderful agricultural and art displays, a floral parade, and sulky races. The Exhibition Hall was a center of activity visited by every fairgoer.

The Nassau Fair flourished until the 1930s when the grounds were used for other activities. In the mid-forties the society joined with the Rensselaer County Agricultural and Horticultural Society in their annual presentation of the Schaghticoke Fair. *Courtesy of the Historical Society of Esquatak*

Founded in 1889 by the Rev. Edward Dudley Tibbitts, the Hoosac School is the only example of a private church-related secondary boarding school in the county. Beginning as a church-choir school for boys, it now functions as a college preparatory school attracting students from many different countries. Its administrative offices are located in the mansion on what was once the Tibbitts estate, the second location for the school.

Hoosac is particularly well known for its Boar's Head and Yule Log Pageant, a regular feature of the school's Christmas celebration since 1892. The rich pageantry of the Hoosac celebration is largely due to the talents and training of Frank Butcher, an organist from Canterbury Cathedral, England, who was brought to Hoosac by Dr. Tibbits, a devoted Anglophile. Finding its inspiration in the medieval celebrations of the winter solstice and incorporating both Christian and pagan traditions, the Hoosac presentation provided the prototype for similar pageants throughout the country. *Courtesy of Hoosac School and Rensselaer County Historical Society*

This fine example of Second Empire architecture at the top of Fulton Street overlooking Troy was built by the Sisters of Charity of St. Vincent de Paul in the late 1860s as the Troy Hospital. In 1923 the building was remodeled to house the new Catholic Central High School formed by the consolidation of the Catholic academies of Troy, Watervliet, and Green Island. The high school remained in the building until 1953 when new buildings in North Troy were purchased to provide more space and a sports field. The old hospital building was then sold to RPI which still uses it under the name of West Hall. *Courtesy of Rensselaer County Historical Society*

One of the most important of the parochial secondary schools in Rensselaer County is the LaSalle Institute, organized in 1847 by Christian brothers as a preparatory school for boys. The mansard-roofed building in the center of this scene was constructed in 1878 to house the school on Fourth Street in Troy. It is now demolished. The two-story building to the left was orginally the school's gymnasium and has been used since then by the Catholic Youth Organization. A recent fire destroyed the interior of the building but with community support it is now being reconstructed. The LaSalle Institute moved to an expansive new facility on Williams Road, North Greenbush in 1966. Today it is a private middle and secondary school with over five hundred students. *Courtesy of Rensselaer County Historical Society*

On a June morning in 1850, a large procession of civic and military dignitaries marched from the Rensselaer County Court House to a field north of the city near Mount Olympus (in the background of the photo) where ground was broken for the Troy and Boston Railroad by Gen. John Wool, Mayor Day Kellogg of Troy, and Amos Briggs of Schaghticoke, president of the company. It was predicted that the tunnel through Hoosac Mountain, the only obstacle along the railroad's route to Boston, would be completed before the railroad from Troy was built to the Vermont line. In fact, the five-mile Hoosac Tunnel wasn't completed until 1875, sixteen years after the tracks reached North Adams, Massachusetts at the tunnel's western portal. This low-level line to Boston competed with the Boston and Albany route through southern Rensselaer County which had steep grades through the Berkshire Mountains, east of the city.

All the necessary facilities for freight handling and locomotive and passenger car servicing were located between Hoosick and Middleburgh streets in North Troy, with a similar freight facility in South Troy at Adams Street. The yards were used well into the twentieth century; here Boston and Maine E7 No. 3800 sits on the turntable in front of the roundhouse at the upper end of the Rensselaer Street yard in North Troy, May 1957. The roundhouse and evidence of the turntable are all that remain of the yard today. *Jim Shaughnessy photo; courtesy of the photographer*

Three J-3a Hudson locomotives were photographed at Rensselaer engine terminal in 1938. These streamlined New York Central steam engines pulled the company's premier passenger train, The Twentieth Century Limited. *Courtesy of Kalmbach Publishing Company*

Chapter Five

1900-1945
Welcome To The Twentieth Century

As the nineteenth century gave way to the twentieth, Rensselaer County residents tried to imagine what new heights her industries could attain. City comforts finally became available to the countryside with the construction of two major new hydroelectric plants on the Hoosic River at Schaghticoke and Valley Falls in the first decade of the century. New York Light and Power built a seven million dollar plant in Troy to provide gas for heating and coke for power generators. Along with electricity came numerous modern devices designed to save labor and provide more time to enjoy the new pleasures of the radio, Victrola and telephone.

Electric trolleys replaced horse-drawn cars and new lines were laid out across the fields. Summer resorts, amusement parks, and cottage colonies developed along the routes as people thronged to escape the city for the countryside. World War I was a sobering experience soon left behind as new inventions and new ideas tumbled America into the modern age. Mass production of automobiles in the 1920s began to transform transportation and leisure activities. No longer were riders tied to a single, set route. Meandering Sunday drives and ad hoc picnics could be taken on purely individual whims. Dine-and-dance halls were a popular destination, even after Prohibition put the brakes on the Roaring Twenties.

The Crash of 1929 and the Depression which followed profoundly affected the county. Many businesses failed, never to revive. The Burden Iron Works in Troy closed in the late 1930s. The Walter A. Wood Mowing and Reaping Machine Company closed in Hoosick Falls, victim of the internal combustion engine which made horse-drawn machinery obsolete. The relentless westward movement of the nation spelled the end of Rensselaer County's preeminence in industry. New sources of raw material in the Midwest, cheaper labor elsewhere, new inventions— all contributed to local factories closing down.

The shirt industry continued to grow for much of the first quarter of the new century, however, and Cluett Peabody and Company, Inc. came to be the largest one of all, employing six thousand people at its height in factories and homes throughout the county. State and federally-funded programs to put people back to work were responsible for numerous bridge-building and road improvement projects.

The outbreak of World War II created a need for all kinds of steel products, clothing, and other locally-produced goods. Republic Steel purchased the Burden Iron Works, only two years after its demise, and other factories geared up to round-the-clock production. Men and women went off to the battlefields, while folks at home made sacrifices daily "for the war effort." The end of the war in 1945 was met with a sigh of relief and hopes of ending the turbulence of the four previous decades.

Poestenkill's turn-of-the-century version of an industrial park stretched alongside the Poestenkill and used the falling water to power its machinery. This double building housed a shirt shop with more than a dozen employees on one side and a wagon-making shop on the other side.

Although today Poestenkill is primarily a bedroom community, it still contains an interesting mix of industries. Duffers Scientific, Inc., a high-tech company, produces the Gleeble which is used by metallurgical labs around the world to simulate and control tests and processes. Another plant, Visilox, is engaged in advanced silicone technology, including special seals for aerospace use, and coatings for computer chips. The unusual list of industries in Poestenkill includes a cosmetics plant, a walking stick company, and a box fabricator, along with a lumber mill, an aggregates operation, and maple sugar production. *Courtesy of Poestenkill Historical Society*

Like Troy, Petersburg developed laundries in association with its shirt factories. The handwork required in making shirts was apt to soil them and laundering also allowed the shirts to be sold "pre-shrunk." In laundries like this one from the early 1900s, gasoline pumps brought water in from the Hoosic River to be heated by immense boilers. The process was not entirely safe; in at least one case, a faulty boiler caused a disastrous fire. To the right of the laundry building is the Petersburg Depot on the Rutland Railroad line connecting the eastern side of the county with Vermont. *Courtesy of Judy Rowe*

The Faith Mills were built in 1897 on the banks of the Wynantskill in Sand Lake. The mill made knit fabrics and garments, using an experienced workforce trained in the several other knitting mills established in that town since the mid-1800s. Workers here produced woolen long underwear during World War II, winning numerous patriotic awards for their contributions to the war effort.

Many people in Sand Lake remember the popular community clubhouse Faith Mills built for their workers and other townspeople in 1919. Bowling alleys, billiards, a restaurant and snack bar were all provided, and upstairs an auditorium and stage were used for the frequent movies and dances, as well as school graduations. *Courtesy of Sand Lake Town Historian*

Elmer Jacobs took this glass plate portrait in the early 1900s of the Lampheres bringing logs to Reuben Lamphere's mill in Grafton. Local forests furnished fine lumber for building, brush blocks, barrels and much more, fueling Rensselaer County's industrial development. The lumber industry was a major employer in the region with loggers coming from Grafton and adjacent mountain communities such as Taborton, Berlin and Poestenkill.

Today Gundrum's Lumber Company in Grafton is typical of ways in which lumbering and logging have grown more sophisticated. Regulations and administrative details, along with the necessary machinery, have become infinitely more complex and expensive. About thirty people are employed at the operation, which specializes in furniture grade hardwoods. *Courtesy of Grafton Historical Society*

Good roads have been in people's thoughts for many years. Long before the interstates were built, survey crews were laying out highways across the county and the state. In this scene from the town of Schodack, even the horse is plugging for "Good Roads." *M. J. Garrison photo; courtesy of Schodack Town Historian*

Shortly before World War I, Frank Brockett and his lumbermen felled a huge tree in Washington County north of Schaghticoke. Measuring 5 feet in diameter at the butt, 3¾ feet at the tip, and 54 feet in length, it was hauled over the frozen ground to Johnsonville on bobsleds pulled by a team of sixteen horses. Relieved that the bridge over the Hoosic River had not collapsed as they crossed it on their way into town, the men and their team paused on Bridge Street for a photographer. The log was displayed in front of Sewels Feed Store until it was sold to the U.S. War Department for use as spud sticks, a tool combining the characteristics of a spade and a chisel, which was used for digging. The Aiken building at right was originally the Episcopal Church. *Courtesy of the Pittstown Historical Society*

Sand, gravel, crushed stone, and clay are all materials necessary for man's built environment. They are the beds of the roads we drive on and the basis of our concrete pavements, dams, and buildings. Rensselaer County is crossed by a number of ridges containing glacial deposits of sand and gravel, and many towns have been able to develop such resources. The Rensselaer Stone Company in Brainard is one good example of the industry. Other firms in the county include Fitzgerald Brothers in Cropseyville, Valente Gravel in Wynantskill, and Bleau Brick in Troy. Poestenkill's quarry on the Plank Road was begun at a place now called "Crusher Hill," and sand and gravel for the roadbed of the railroad was found next to the line in Berlin. *Courtesy of the Historical Society of Esquatak*

In more rural parts of the state and in earlier generations, merchants often doubled up on the services which they provided their customers. It was not particularly uncommon, for instance, for the local cabinetmaker to also produce coffins as needed. This seems to be the case at Porter Lamphier's store on Railroad Avenue across the tracks from Berlin's train station in the early 1900s. In later years the Rensselaer County Highway Department used this building for storage. *Courtesy of Berlin Historical Society*

Rensselaer County's people, events, and buildings have been documented by many photographers. This was Henry Austin's studio on South Main Street, Berlin. The building was Derby's blacksmith shop prior to its use as Austin's studio; it no longer exists. *Henry Austin photo; courtesy of Berlin Historical Society*

The Colonial Inn has watched many changes in Berlin since Burton Hammond first built it in 1806. Over the years it has been called Hammond's Hotel, Niles's Hotel, Berlin Hotel, and the Taconic Inn. The building is still standing and now is used as a restaurant.

Like much of the eastern half of Rensselaer County, Berlin was settled by large numbers of New England farmers. Industry began quickly to accommodate the needs of the new settlers with a sawmill, gristmill, and smithy opening up around 1780.

By the mid-nineteenth century James L. Green's foundry was turning out cast iron fences, plows and other farm implements. The Saterlee Cheese Company produced twenty-two thousand pounds of cheese in June 1904. At its centennial in 1906, Berlin may have been at its industrial and commercial peak. A town publication lists these establishments in 1906: a milk condensery, milk station, creamery, sawmill, smithies, a shirt factory and laundry employing eighty persons each, and eight stores in addition to a barber, cobbler, dressmaker, and milliner; lumber, coal and wood dealers; tobacco and ice cream shops. The flower and wood products industries, the two leading businesses in Berlin today, were in their early stages. *Courtesy of Berlin Town Historian*

A photograph of the interior of Castleton-on-Hudson's National Savings Bank around 1920 shows the many changes in banking which have taken place since that time. The ornate wallpaper and heavily carved wood-work are typical of early twentieth-century interiors, as is the combination gas/electric light fixture. The tellers on duty are LeRoy Bridenbeck, leaning on one of the voluminous ledger books used for accounts, and George Schermerhorn, who later became the bank's president. In 1924 National Savings Bank moved to its present building and this office on Main Street became a private home which still stands today. *Courtesy of Castleton-on-Hudson Village Archives*

In the early 1900s many small farmers sold their milk to local creameries where the milk was separated and bottled or made into butter, buttermilk, cottage cheese, and (at Thurston's Creamery in Brunswick) ice cream. Creameries also bought cream from farmers who collected it on regular routes. Individual farm families separated the cream for sale, keeping the milk for use at home or feeding it to their hogs. Creameries sold their dairy products to peddlers, stores, and individuals. This Brunswick creamery on Moonlawn Road is now a private residence. *Courtesy of Brunswick Historical Society*

As the century progressed, creameries became increasingly more mechanized. Here is Howard Chittenden at work in this Stephentown creamery in the 1920s. *Courtesy of Stephentown Historical Society*

Tomhannock Reservoir in Pittstown, five-and-a-half miles in length and up to two miles in width, is the largest source of water in the county. It supplies Troy so abundantly that the city sells water to Menands and Rensselaer, portions of Brunswick and East Greenbush, and sometimes to Waterford. In 1900 the Troy Water Works started plans to create the reservoir by accessioning 1,700 acres and eighty homesites. An eight-mile pipeline was extended to Troy and the new water supply was turned on May 21, 1906. Eventually the whole water supply for the city came from the Tomhannock, replacing the Grafton chain of lakes, now part of Grafton Lakes State Park, in that capacity. *Gene Baxter photo; courtesy of the* Times Record

Some of Pittstown's most beautiful farmland was covered forever when the reservoir was built. While some of the displaced farmers took their money and left farming altogether, others bought new lands where three and four generations of the family continue to work the land. *Courtesy of Pittstown Town Historian*

The Johnsonville Dam, a solid concrete dam forty feet high and eight hundred feet long, was built in 1906 to replace the old mill dam across the Hoosic River on the same site. It forms a reservoir of eighteen hundred acres, backing water upstream seven miles to Buskirk. The reservoir also feeds the larger power plant at Schaghticoke and the electric power from both plants was originally transmitted to the General Electric Company in Schenectady. It is now used by Niagara Mohawk. *Courtesy of Pittstown Historical Society*

For almost a hundred years, Troy's shopping crowds ebbed and flowed through Frear's dry goods store. By 1900 Frear's Troy Cash Bazaar was one of the largest department stores in a state full of large mercantile establishments.

William H. Frear came to Troy in 1859 to work in a dry goods store. By 1874 he was sole owner of the prosperous Cannon Building. In 1897 he began to build the familiar edifice at Third and Fulton streets. Designed by Mortimer L. Smith and Sons of Detroit, the store was filled with artwork and had an ornate interior staircase topped by a leaded glass skylight. Frear's transacted a million-dollars-per-year mail order business and is said to have coined the phrase "satisfaction guaranteed or your money back." The exterior and lower stories of the building were recently restored and provide both commercial and office spaces. *Courtesy of Rensselaer County Historical Society*

For nearly a century and a half, railroads were the giants of American industry and a major force in the development of the American continent. In practically every community, from the most obscure water stop to the large cities, the railroad station was a focus of activity and of civic pride. Railway companies realized the importance of the railway station and lavished the best design and architecture on them. Troy Union Station was no exception.

The St. Paul firm of Reed and Stern in collaboration with New York Central's brilliant engineering vice president, William J. Wilgus, designed the station. The firm won a competition to design New York City's Grand Central Terminal shortly after they completed Troy Union Station in 1902. The station's grand lobby was recorded by Troy

commercial photographer Bert Boice about 1915. A railway official, "Keystone Cop," and porter pose by the subway entrance near the floor compass. Behind them a poster advertises an excursion fare to New York on Sundays or holidays at $2.50 round trip.

The last train to New York left Troy on January 5, 1958 and the last Boston and Maine train pulled out thirteen days later. Efforts to adaptively reuse the depot were unsuccessful and it fell to the wreckers the same year. As a final irony, the station site was used for many years as a parking lot.

In 1968 the Holiday Inn was built on the east side of the old main tracks, which are now Sixth Avenue, and in 1974, the Raddeck Building was built on the depot's site.
Courtesy of Rensselaer County Historical Society

The Ilium Building, designed by Frederick M. Cummings at the northeast corner of Fourth and Fulton streets, housed Thomas McBride's tailor shop and hattery, Wagar's ice cream, and others on the ground floor. The local office of the Prudential Insurance and the Artistic Shirt Company factory occupied the upper floors. The building, constructed about 1904, incorporated the best of modern building technology with the supposedly fireproof iron frames and masonry curtain walls. The National State Bank at 297 River Street stood nearby; the two buildings were Troy's first skyscrapers, both built by the same architect in the same year. *Courtesy of Rensselaer County Historical Society*

Through the years fires continued to be a major foe of the city. In Troy, the Boardman Building, a large four-story structure at Fulton and River streets across from William H. Frear's department store, went up in flames on January 26, 1911. A falling wall killed Lt. Edward J. Butler of Truck No. 2. The building, leveled by the fire, had once contained the Boston Department Store on the first floor and the Troy Rubber Stamp Works on the second floor. *Courtesy of Joseph A. Parker*

The Troy Record Building was completed in 1909 at Broadway and Fifth Avenue. At that time Troy was distinctive among cities of its size in having ten newspapers. Besides the *Troy Record*, there were the *Troy Daily Press*, the *Evening Standard*, the *Troy Times*, the *Troy Northern Budget*, the *Observer*, the *Sunday Telegram*, the *Labor Advocate, Troy Freie Press* (a German language paper), and *Saturday Globe.* In addition, there were many smaller publications, mostly weeklies, which thrived in the various towns and villages. Lansingburgh published the earliest newspaper in the county, the *Northern Centinel* in 1786.

The 1935 merger of the *Troy Times* with the *Troy Record* left only one daily newspaper in the city. In 1972 Harry Horvitz, who then owned four Ohio newspapers, purchased the locally-owned newspaper. He sold his newspapers to the Ingersoll newspaper chain in 1987. Despite the changes, the now regional newspaper retains its editorial independence. *Courtesy of Rensselaer County Historical Society*

Transportation history between Rensselaer County (along the top of this photo in what is now the city of Rensselaer) and the opposite riverbank at Albany can be traced back to 1642, when the first ferry at Greenbush was established. Just to the north at Bath-on-Hudson, the newly constructed Boston and Albany Railroad established its own ferry in 1842. Strong opposition from Troy and Lansingburgh interests prevented construction of a bridge at Albany until 1866, when a railroad bridge was completed near the present Amtrak/Conrail bridge. A railroad and foot bridge (at right in photo) opened in 1872, and a toll bridge for teams and foot passengers opened in 1882 to the south. Looking across the Albany boat basin beyond several docked steamers is the Hudson Navigation Company's *Rensselaer,* which carried passengers and their autos overnight to Pier 32 in New York City. Launched in 1909, it ran until the end of the 1930s. The railroad's speed and all-weather efficiency, and the ever growing numbers of automobiles spelled the doom of the Hudson steamers. The last regularly scheduled steamboat to traverse the river left Albany on September 3, 1948 and ended an era on the Hudson. The shop complexes, bridge, and boat basin in this photo have long since vanished. *Courtesy of G. Steven Draper*

Early in this century, the "palatial steamers" of the Hudson River Dayline, the Citizens' Steamboat Company, and the Hudson Navigation Company, traversed what was advertised as the "most charming inland water trip on the American continent." At its height, travel by steamboat was pleasant and luxurious, whether by day or night. Passengers could travel in plush gaslit parlors, lavish dining rooms, or airy staterooms high above the water's surface. In addition to the big steamship lines, there were smaller companies that served the tiny communities along the Hudson. The river steamers had the joint character of commuter vessels and excursion boats. Here is the *A. J. Phillips* at Castleton-on-Hudson around 1915. The Catskill and Albany Steamboat Company provided local service along the river, including stops at Cedar Hill, Coeymans, and New Baltimore. *Courtesy of Castleton-on-Hudson Village Archives*

The electric interurban line was an American transportation phenomenon. Evolved from the urban steetcar, interurban lines appeared shortly before the dawn of this century and grew to a vast network of over eighteen thousand miles in two decades of exuberant growth. They all but vanished after nearly three decades of usefulness, due to improved roads and the increased use of automobiles. Rensselaer County was traversed by several lines. The line from Hoosick Falls to Bennington connected for a short time with a network of trolley rails running all the way to Boston. The Albany Hudson "Fast Line" interurban served communities along its route through southern Rensselaer County. In 1929, the last year of its operation, the commute from East Schodack to Albany's Delaware and Hudson Plaza was a quick thirty minutes by rail, including stops at East Greenbush and Rensselaer. A Troy and New England Railway construction crew posed for the camera while they were working on the line between Albia and Averill Park. Service along the picturesque route began September 30, 1895, and ended in March 1925. *Courtesy of Charles Viens*

Trolley rides and picnics were popular forms of Saturday and Sunday entertainment. One of the most popular trolley lines, the Troy and New England, provided a ready access to Snyders Lake, Brookside Park, Crystal Lake, Averill Park and the many lakes of Sand Lake. The Averill Park Land Improvement Company, promoters of the railway, acquired more than three hundred acres in the village of Averill Park and its environs to develop a summer resort of hotels and summer homes as well as permanent homes in the early years of this century. It managed the Averill Park Hotel and Sunset Lodge with every amenity and promised a quiet and restful time to all who participated in their venture. The photographer stopped these travelers at the Averill Park "end of the line" depot with its cast-iron ornamentation. *Courtesy of Jim Shaughnessy*

In the late summer of 1909, the whole Hudson Valley celebrated two anniversaries important to its river heritage: the 300 years since Henry Hudson discovered the river named after him, and the 102 years since Robert Fulton invented a successful steamboat. There were grand celebrations in communities along the river in Rensselaer County as buildings were decorated for massive parades and shorelines jammed with people to watch the flotilla of boats pass. Included was a replica of both Fulton's *North River Steamboat* (later called *Clermont*) and Henry Hudson's *Halfmoon.* The Hudson-Fulton Celebration fleet is seen here at Troy looking towards the Congress Street Bridge. *Courtesy of Troy Public Library*

Hanging on to your hat was a requirement when riding the roller coaster at Rensselaer Park in Lansingburgh. This park was a real "Tivoli" at the turn of the century with its many fun rides, concessions, booths and games, a racing track, and pavilions for exhibitions, concerts and various meetings of organizations and societies. The park was closed down in the 1920s to become a new housing site. The famous carousel was moved to Crystal Lake Park in Averill Park where it was enjoyed by young and old for many years. It was then moved to Halfmoon Beach where it was subsequently dismantled and sold out of the area. *Courtesy of Frances D. Broderick*

Snyder's Lake, the first "lake" stop on the Troy and New England Railway, was a favorite recreation area on the trolley due to its proximity to the Capital District. Numerous cottages were built in the earlier years for city dwellers to escape to during the summer. Many have been converted to permanent homes and today the lake is enjoyed year round. Camp Scully, a children's day and sleep-away camp, and the North Greenbush Town Beach are both situated on the lake. *Courtesy of Rensselaer County Historical Society*

The Lansingburgh section of Troy has a long history of boat building. Soon after the turn of the century, a small company was building these wooden gasoline-powered boats. An unusual feature of these small pleasure boats was a "convertible top," probably with roll-down canvas sides for inclement weather. *Courtesy of Frances D. Broderick*

At the end of the nineteenth century, a public movement began to call for the establishment in Troy of some public parks. In response to this, Frear Park—nearly two hundred acres in size—was purchased as well as lands in the center of the city which would become Prospect Park. Eighty-four acres of Warren family property on the top of Mount Ida were purchased in 1903 and laid out in winding walks and elaborate flower beds with a lake and a scenic overlook constructed looking out over the city. The entire plan was created by Garnet D. Baltimore, a landscape engineer who was RPI's first black graduate in 1891. Baltimore worked as city engineer for a number of years. In addition to Prospect Park, he designed the landscaping and engineering of St. Mary's Hospital as well as cemeteries in Albany, Amsterdam, Hoosick Falls, Glens Falls and Forest Park, Brunswick (now reputed to be the most haunted cemetery in the country). Baltimore also served as consulting engineer for the Oakwood Cemetery for thirty years.

In the 1930s a municipal swimming pool with an outstanding program for children and adults was built at the park. Hundreds have learned to swim here. The city has also added pools at two other sites, Lansingburgh's Knickerbocker Park and South Troy. *Courtesy of Rensselaer County Historical Society*

The Troy Times Fresh Air Fund was established in 1887 to provide summer vacations in the country for less-privileged city children. In 1908 the Tilley farm and fifty acres were purchased in East Grafton for a home base, opening for use in 1909. The home was enlarged and other buildings added. Each summer hundreds of city children had vacations of a week or more, and as more rooms were added, working mothers were often allowed to have a vacation along with their children. The program was supported by the newspaper and private citizens. As with many programs, costs became prohibitive and the lack of support as well as governmental interference, affected the continuance of such a fine program. *Courtesy of Rensselaer County Historical Society*

Before World War I it was comparatively easy to get to this resort at East Schodack from Albany or New York City by following the directions on the business card. Stop 77 was 7.7 miles from Albany. Rheingold's catered to Jewish clientele as did other hotels and boarding houses in the Nassau area. Many Jewish families of Russian extraction settled in this region in the early part of the twentieth century. They started farms, built synagogues, boarding houses, and hotels which attracted Jewish patronage, particularly during the summer months.

In 1927 LaSalle School of Albany purchased the property and started a summer camp which is still active today. *Courtesy of Rensselaer County Historical Society*

The whole city turned out for a parade in 1918 to welcome home Troy's 105th Regiment from their service in the Great War. The soldiers and bands were cheered by well-wishers as they marched down Third Street. This view catches the crowds gathered across the street from the old City Hall at Third and State streets.

All the towns in Rensselaer County sent young men off to Europe during World War I to fight "the war to end all wars." Unfortunately, future generations of Rensselaer County would have to answer similar calls to fight in three more major wars during the twentieth century. *Courtesy of Joseph A. Parker*

Freihofer's Bakery, at 125th Street, was the home of the horse-drawn delivery wagons that daily plied the streets of Troy and many other towns. According to company folk history, Charles Freihofer stopped in Troy on a trip to Montreal. Upon learning that Troy's industries employed so many women (particularly in the collar trades), Freihofer sensed a market for providing fresh bread for working women. He sent his three sons up to Troy from their Philadelphia bakery that same year, 1913. Freihofer's home delivery service was a key part of their services for over fifty years. In 1962, the last of the horse-drawn vehicles was retired, and ten years later the company made its last home delivery in the area. On August 19, 1987, Freihofer's had agreed in principle to accept a purchase offer from General Foods. No change in their relationship with the community is anticipated. *Courtesy of Frances D. Broderick*

Horses, unlike the machines that replaced them, had distinctive personalities. They were a crucial part of Rensselaer County's agriculture, commerce and industry. Sometimes they even made the newspaper. Here are pictured the favorite horses of Troy's fire department, as published in the 1913 January-June *Pictorial Review* by the Troy Standard Press. Among them were Hank, Souse, and Dan. Lobster and Frank (lower right) were the oldest team in the department. The paper indicated that Chief (6) formerly of the Bussey Engine Company, had recently been sold in New York, but there was no indication of what "sold in New York" actually meant. *Courtesy of Rensselaer County Historical Society*

The "horseless carriage," at first available to only the rich, was to become affordable for most people. This new machine created its own service industries, which still exist today. This was the scene at Clum's Corners in Brunswick at Routes 2 and 278 in the early 1900s. The building at left is a blacksmith shop. Judging from the variety of vehicles shown, the blacksmith has already begun to transfer his skills to horseless carriages. *Courtesy of Brunswick Historical Society*

Charles J. Vannier started a carriage works in Whitehall, New York about 1900. He came to Troy a short time later and, as a partner of Mr. Davis, opened this carriage shop at 2748 Sixth Avenue. It was a time of transition; Stillman Betts's horse stable was still in operation just down the block, but Vannier was quickly called on to translate his painting, upholstery and carriage repair skills to the growing numbers of fine autos and trucks, as well as delivery wagons. Owners of the horse-drawn wagons could count on Vannier and his crew to make or repair any wagon part, but at the same time owners of early 1900s trucks, such as Bulldog Mack Trucks, came to him for fine painting and striping. At one time Packard automobiles were delivered to Vannier's shop with a primer coat only, and his grandson still remembers the grand sight of a whole fleet of finished Packards in the front yard, beautifully custom-painted and striped. Some time after Vannier's death the business was sold, about 1929. The building is now owned by Collin Lumber Corp. *Courtesy of Walter Catricala*

The Rensselaer County sheriff's office and the county jail behind it were built in 1912. The two buildings replaced a structure built in 1826 on the same northeast corner of Fifth Avenue and Ferry Street. The county's first jail was rather small, and it stood behind the courthouse at Congress and Second streets. Outmoded for the needs of the 1980s, the present jail is currently center of an extended debate concerning its renovation or totally new construction. *Thomas Killips photo; courtesy of the* Times Record

Early bus travel was not noted for comfort. This bus belonged to the "Troy-Grafton Auto Line," managed by E. L. Snyder. Note the canvas curtains which were rolled down if the weather turned foul. This photo was taken about 1909. *Gene Baxter photo; courtesy of Keith Marvin*

Fire Chief Philip King (in white hat) proudly stands on the running board of a 1919 Federal truck which was Rensselaer's Pumper No. 4. The vehicle was the city's first motorized fire truck. Within ten years the old horse-drawn fire engines had almost all been replaced in towns throughout the county. *Courtesy of Rensselaer County Historical Society*

South of Rensselaer, interurban trains of the Albany Southern Railroad raced down the east side of the Hudson to East Schodack, Nassau, and Kinderhook on their way to the New York Central Depot at Hudson. For several summers the line offered a combination jaunt, one-way on the interurban and return via Hudson River steamer for seventy-five cents. Its freight business served industries along the line, such as the piano action factory at Nassau, and the grain warehouse and cider mill at East Schodack. Albany Southern owned the Albany and Greenbush toll bridge, later sold to the state, and all the gas and electric lighting plants in Hudson and Rensselaer which served southern Rensselaer County.

In winter the railroad fought an ongoing battle with snow as evidenced by this photo taken in February 1920. Note the electrified "third rail" which powered the trains and was the object of many interesting encounters, both human and animal.

"If any living thing was plagued by the third rail, it was the dogs that lived along the Albany Southern. Male dogs particularly would saunter up to the track and casually lift their hind leg. Usually, it was their last act on this earth, but there's the story of a Kinderhook dog that survived the leg-lifting episode but became so infuriated that he bit the third rail in retaliation, a reaction he failed to survive" (Gordon, *Third Rail*). The line did not survive either after 1927, but its tracks can still be traced. *Courtesy of Schodack Town Historian*

The control and regulation of the Hudson River's Adirondack watershed was first proposed in 1895 to prevent the chronic cycles of flooding and drought that plagued the Hudson River Valley. The riverfront communities of Lansingburgh, Troy, Rensselaer, and Castleton-on-Hudson were periodically inundated, as were those along other rivers and streams. Pictured is Castleton's main street about 1902, and Troy's Franklin Square in 1913. By 1930, the Hudson River Regulating District, established eight years earlier, had completed the Conklingville Dam on the Sacandaga River, thus controlling the floods. The resulting forty-two-square-mile body of water is the largest working reservoir in New York State. The cost of the reservoir's maintenance is borne by public and private entities downstream. *Courtesy of Castleton-on-Hudson Village Archives and Rensselaer County Historical Society*

By the time this 1928 photograph was taken, Troy was laced with a network of trolley tracks and overhead power lines. The view down Fourth Street from Division Street northward toward Ferry Street was typical with its many poles and vintage cars. Today the tracks and trolley are gone, and the overhead wires have all been buried in underground conduits. Many of the buildings still remain, among them Ehrlich's Auto Supply Store which continues to do business at the same site. *McKenna photo; courtesy of Keith Marvin*

This United Traction Company trolley car ran on the Watervliet-Troy Belt Line No. 15. It was built by the Jones Trolley Car Company in Watervliet in 1900. The picture was taken in 1929 in front of the big trolley barn at the end of Second Avenue opposite the Waterford Bridge. The Troy and Lansingburgh Horse Railway opened here in 1860 and was extended to the Burden Iron Works in 1861. The line was electrified in 1889 as part of the Troy City Railway. The car barn, built in 1900, also housed the interurban cars of the Hudson Valley Railway, which operated to Saratoga, Lake George, and Warrensburg. J. M. Fields Department Store occupied the building later, and it is presently unoccupied. A similar structure in Rensselaer, also a car barn, is now a toy store. *Courtesy of Keith Marvin*

When erected in Troy in 1914, Proctor's Theater was the largest of F. F. Proctor's vaudeville theater chain. Seating more than twenty-five hundred, it was luxurious in its interior with much gilt and many murals by the famed area artist, David Lithgow. It had every modern accessory including a theater organ and a stage eighty-five feet wide by forty feet deep. The vaudeville shows here included the best performers in the country. When talking pictures eventually replaced vaudeville, Proctor's converted to a movie house and continued to operate until the popularity of television caused its closing in 1977. For a number of years fifteen movie theaters provided entertainment for people in the greater Troy area.

Throughout the county, each community seemed to have a place for showing movies. Some had separate movie theaters while others used the Town Hall, the Grange Hall, the Knights of Columbus, or Masonic halls, or any meeting place that could provide seating, a power supply, and a screen. *Courtesy of Rensselaer County Historical Society*

These women are seated before the stage of the Eagle Opera House at the Head of the Lane, Petersburg about 1900. The "opera house" played an important part in the activities of many towns and villages throughout the county. The elaborately painted scenic curtain in this Petersburg theater was made by the Huiest Theatrical Scenery Company of Lansingburgh. A number of the opera houses and theaters in the county had scenery created by this local company. *Courtesy of Nancy Bernstein*

William Phibbs erected the opera house at 60 Main Street, Castleton-on-Hudson around 1899. Through the years the building has been a theater and movie house, with shops on the main floor. It has served as a church and in the 1970s was owned by the Independent Order of Odd Fellows for its meetings. The same can be said of many "opera houses" throughout the county. They were the place for home town theatricals, traveling shows, Chautauquas, revivals, lectures, and musicals, not to mention an occasional school graduation or wedding reception. *Courtesy of Castleton-on-Hudson Village Archives*

Rensselaer County has had a number of unusual industries over the years. Soon after moving to Schodack in 1837, Frederick Frickinger engaged workmen, some from his native Germany, and practiced the skill for which he had become known in New York City—making custom-built pianos with superior actions and notable tone. In 1875 he built a three-story factory for making the piano actions only, which he then sold to piano makers.

After his retirement Frickinger gave the factory to two employees, William Gorgen and Jacob Grubb. Gorgen opened another piano action factory in Castleton-on-Hudson, and sold his interest in the Schodack factory to three brothers who had also learned the piano action business as Frickinger's apprentices: Albrecht, Otto, and Charles Kosegarten. Grubb and Kosegarten Brothers produced piano actions in their mentor's factory until it burned to the ground in 1904. Within six months the factory was rebuilt in the nearby village of Nassau. After Jacob Grubb's death less than two years later, the Kosegarten brothers continued the business and are shown here in their office around 1910.

At its peak the Kosegarten factory employed 165 people and produced thirty-five thousand piano actions per year. These were sold to piano makers in the United States, Canada, and Great Britain. Times changed, however, and pianos were no longer found in every parlor, nor needed for entertainment. The Kosegarten Piano Action Manufacturing Company liquidated in 1929 and the factory has been converted into apartments. *Elmer Shaver photo; courtesy of Mary and Herman Kosegarten*

Farmers not only raise crops and cattle, they raise barns for other farmers as these men are doing at the Pratt Farm on Phillips Road, East Greenbush. The barn is now a home. All over the county farmers are known for the help they offer to their neighbors. *Courtesy of East Greenbush Town Historian*

In the early years of this century, visitors thronged to Berlin annually to see a dazzling display: fifty varieties of gladiolas in full bloom, covering about one hundred acres at Arthur Cowee's gladiola farm. Migrant workers assisted local work crews in planting and digging the bulbs in fields stretching along the Little Hoosic River and in Southeast Hollow. From Cowee's storehouse near the Berlin railroad station, carloads of cut flowers and prize-winning bulbs were shipped all over the United States for more than fifteen years. *Courtesy of Berlin Town Historian*

Catalogue
1904
OF
GROFF'S
NEW
Hybrid Gladioli
TOGETHER WITH OTHER VARIETIES
OF ACKNOWLEDGED MERIT.

ARTHUR COWEE
MEADOWVALE FARM, BERLIN, N.Y.

Agriculture continued to be a major occupation for Rensselaer County residents in the first half of the twentieth century. Abram and LeGrand Whyland stopped for the camera on a pre-1920 summer day as they were cutting corn at the Whyland farm on the Poestenkill-Cropseyville Road. The land is now part of the Schmidt farm. *Courtesy of Poestenkill Town Historian*

A youngster shows off prize vegetables on his grandfather John W. Sliter's farm on Vly Road in North Greenbush about 1924. Mr. Sliter peddled milk from his dairy farm for sixty-five years, as well as cabbages and other vegetables. The truck is a Hupmobile, with gravity gas feed from the tank atop the dashboard. *Courtesy of John E. Finegan*

Typical of the many gasoline stations that sprang up in the period from 1915 to 1935, this Colonial Gas pump was located at John Bubie's General Store, a Poestenkill landmark since the early 1900s. Bubie's moved from this location about forty years ago to the former Woodbine Hotel, where it still exists. *Courtesy of Frederick Reichard*

In the first decades of the twentieth century, new homes continued to be built in neighborhoods along the edges of the cities. Served by trolley lines or bus routes, the houses had ample yards where residents, many originally from more rural areas of the county, planted large gardens for their own larders. A flock of chickens like those being fed by Clara Texter and her daughters, Pearl and Gladys, was not unusual. They were photographed about 1920 in East Greenbush Terrace. This early subdivision had its own water supply from wells that are still being used by the town. *Courtesy of East Greenbush Town Historian*

Prize cattle lined up for their picture around 1945 at one of Brunswick's many large dairy farms. Originally the Clum-Eddy farm, this complex was then owned by Horace Dunham and called Dunshire Farms, where he raised these champion Ayreshires. Dunham's cows were bred to produce milk with high butterfat content, a characteristic not so important in these calorie-conscious days. The farm was later known as Langmoore, when owned by the Moore family, and today the barn has become a local bar. *Courtesy of Rensselaer County Historical Society*

Hay continued to be an excellent cash crop for Rensselaer County farmers well into the 1930s. "Teams were on the road all the time, drawing hay and straw to the city," one farmer says, explaining that a multitude of delivery wagons—for coal and wood, bakery products, milk and ice, to name a few—used horse power, and thus required endless tons of hay and straw for feed and bedding. Many people recall being in the procession of automobiles behind a hay wagon, like this one on the Poestenkill-Cropseyville Road, unable to find a place to pass! *Courtesy of Frederick Reichard*

This popular type of summer cottage with board-and-batten siding and wide verandas with awnings for extra shade overlooked Vanderheyden Reservoir in Brunswick. These ladies are enjoying a quiet afternoon with one another in July 1925, creating a scene common among summer residents. A nice chat was almost always accompanied by some knitting, tatting, crocheting, or other kind of handwork. *P. Knudsen photo; courtesy of Robert N. Andersen*

This 1923 summer scene is a family picnic in the country near East Schodack. Such outings were often recorded using the trusted Kodak Brownie camera, one of which can be seen in the left foreground. In good weather the open touring car was a delight for drives in the country but when a storm came, quick hands arranged side curtains on the car to keep rain out. In winter months, the touring car was usually put up on blocks and garaged until spring. *N. P. Andersen photo; courtesy of Robert N. Andersen*

In color, the theme would be red, white, and blue for this female group prepared to join the Fourth of July Parade in Berlin, 1920. Parades were amalgamators of county communities and almost every holiday featured a parade of some sort. Even conventions and special meetings of organizations, unions, and schools quite often ended in a parade. To quote a popular song of the day, it seems that everyone "loves a parade." *Courtesy of Rensselaer County Historical Society*

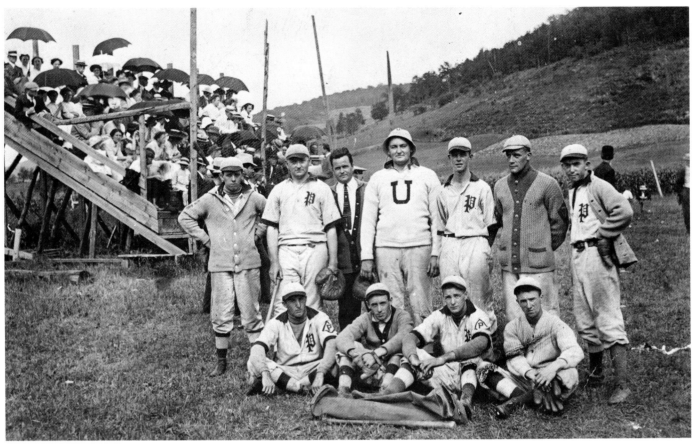

Every town and village of size in Rensselaer County had a baseball team. This Petersburg team is properly uniformed even to the well-labeled umpire. Spectators came prepared for summer sun or an unexpected rain shower. Judging by the happy faces, this was no doubt a winning team. *Courtesy of Judy Rowe*

A well-known boys' camp at Burden Lake was Camp Van Schoonhoven. Dedicated in July 1921 as a memorial to Francis Y. Van Schoonhoven, it was given by his sisters to the Troy YMCA. The ninety-acre farm had accommodations for more than sixty boys with a lodge, dining hall and cook shack, and numerous tent-cabins for eight boys each. There was an athletic field for games, tennis courts, volleyball courts, and all kinds of waterfront equipment on the beautiful site located on a high bluff going right to the lake shore. Changes in lifestyle and the high cost of upkeep ultimately caused the camp to close. *Courtesy of Rensselaer County Historical Society*

Totem Lodge on Burden Lake in Nassau was Rensselaer County's biggest summer resort for many years. The site began as the hundred-acre Camp Totem, summer home of Matthew Larkin. In 1922, Nathan Naum and Jacob Bashein of New York City purchased it, plus many adjoining acres for the resort. Totem Lodge could house more than seven hundred guests in its lodges and cottages. It had a great indoor swimming pool as well as a lake beach, a nine-hole golf course and almost every type of game and sport available. The nightclub-theater seated one thousand and featured famous top-bill entertainers. The lodge was known for good cuisine. Totem Lodge closed about 1958, but the golf course has since been revived and the rest of the property is being developed into luxury, year-round housing. *Courtesy of Sand Lake Town Historian*

The 1911 establishment of Troop No. 1 in Troy marks the beginning of Rensselaer County's participation in the Boy Scouts of America. Troop No. 1 was among the first officially recognized Boy Scout units and was the first uniformed Boy Scout troop in the United States. The uniform was designed by Charles M. Connolly of Troy and manufactured by Cluett Peabody. A photograph of that troop was published in the first edition of the *Boy Scouts of America Manual.* Scouting became popular and by 1925 there were twenty-seven troops in the county. This is Troop No. 16 (now 516) at School 18, posing with their scout master, Harold H. Tice, about 1927.

Camp Rotary at Davitt's Lake in Poestenkill was a gift to Rensselaer County Boy Scouts from the Troy Rotary Club in 1923. It is still actively used by local Boy Scouts. In the decades since World War II scouting has added activities for youth of earlier ages and offers many different programs. Today there are nineteen troops within the county. *Courtesy of LeRoy Johnson, Sr.*

Troy School of Arts and Crafts was located in the Hannibal Green building on Broadway. Organized in 1908 at the peak of the arts and crafts movement, it had eight rooms devoted to many areas of art study, including sketching, several types of painting, wood carving, basketry, jewelry and metal working, enameling, tatting, and embroidery. Courses were open to men, women, and children. The staff of five instructors, along with the director, Miss Emilie C. Adams, were all former faculty members of the Emma Willard Art School. *Courtesy of Rensselaer County Historical Society*

In 1904 a fire destroyed two of RPI's buildings. There was talk of relocating to Columbia University in New York City, but both alumni and local citizens wanted it kept here. At a cost of forty thousand dollars, the city built this approach to recognize a link between the city and the school and perhaps to overcome the town-gown antagonism which existed because of tax-exempt buildings. For years student classes had their pictures taken on the stairway. This class may have come directly from the Walker Labora-tory, because they are still wearing their protective aprons. Unfortunately, the approach eventually began to deteriorate. A joint effort between RPI and Troy is under way to renovate the steps. *Courtesy of Rensselaer Polytechnic Institute Archives*

Students at Emma Willard were encouraged to participate in such activities as fencing and gymnastics. These young fencers squared off in an old schoolroom a few short years before they moved up the hill to their new campus.

A spacious new campus on Pawling Avenue was built in 1910, providing students with the best in educational facilities. Funding for the new campus came primarily from Olivia Sage, an alumna of Emma Willard in the days when the school was still known as the Troy Female Seminary.

On her way to Mount Holyoke Seminary in the 1840s, Margaret Olivia Slocum had become ill and stopped to stay with her uncle in Troy. He suggested she might consider attending the Troy Female Seminary instead. She did and graduated in 1846, later marrying Russell Sage, a wealthy financier and businessman.

After the death of her husband, Olivia Sage became one of the area's leading philanthropists. After providing funds for a new campus for Emma Willard School, Mrs. Sage was concerned that the old buildings on the downtown campus be reused. Believing there was a need for education for young women which would allow them to earn a living, she founded Russell Sage College to train teachers. *Courtesy of Emma Willard Archives*

Founded in 1907 and accredited by the state, the Berlin High School had the distinction in 1912 and 1913 of holding training classes for teachers and sending eleven teachers out into the district. Students used the school on North Main Street until 1937 when the Berlin Central School District was formed and a new school building constructed on School Street.

The classrooms of the old Berlin High School, pictured in use around 1921, were later converted to apartments. The building was destroyed in a gas explosion in 1962. *Courtesy of Berlin Historical Society*

The original Hoosick Falls High School was built in 1885 and used until 1927 when the town converted the Walter A. Wood mansion into library, offices and classrooms, and added a new wing of additional classrooms and a gymnasium. This building was abandoned and later torn down in the 1960s when the local schools were further centralized and a single large school for grades K-12 was built on the west edge of the town. *Courtesy of William Andrick*

143

"The Little Red Schoolhouse" in the Williams District of North Greenbush is still in use for primary grades. Built in 1886, it is probably the only one-room schoolhouse in Rensselaer County still being used for its original purpose. While the children's faces have changed from those in this 1936 photograph and the big stove is gone, children still cut out pictures of pumpkins around Halloween, and the familiar faces of George Washington and Abraham Lincoln still look down from the walls. *Courtesy of Rensselaer County Historical Society*

This brand new Troy Fifth Avenue Bus arrived in about 1929. The body was built in Poughkeepsie by Guilder on a Mack chassis. It only cost a nickel to take the bus then. The Fifth Avenue Line, from the end of Lansingburgh to downtown Troy, was noted for good service and it ran frequently. Riders only waited five to ten minutes before the next bus arrived. *Courtesy of John Peckham*

You would have to be an old timer to remember Troy's traffic tower at the city's busiest intersection—Third, River, and Fulton streets. The photo was taken from Frear's corner looking toward Peerless's Store. The tower was torn down sometime in the late 1930s and replaced by a traffic light. *Courtesy of Keith Marvin*

Even with two separate railroad bridges spanning the Hudson River at Albany and four tracks up West Albany hill, the New York Central Railroad was bottlenecked in Rensselaer County. To alleviate the congestion, the New York Central Railroad constructed the "Castleton cutoff" at a cost of twenty-five million dollars, completed in 1924. Work included a new bridge over a mile in length across the Hudson Valley below Castleton-on-Hudson and a huge new classification freight yard and shops at Selkirk in Albany County. Financed entirely with corporation funds (federal subsidies weren't an option then), the line branched off from the old Boston and Albany main at Post Road Crossing in southern Rensselaer County and connected with the West Shore Railroad across the river. Since the burning of the Poughkeepsie bridge in 1974, the A. H. Smith Memorial Bridge has become the major artery for freight to and from New England. *Courtesy of Kalmbach Publishing Company*

In Troy almost a mile and a half of land beside the Hudson River from Adams Street south to the Menands Bridge was occupied by major industrial complexes which produced iron and steel for over a century. These plants were operated by four major groups: the Albany Iron Works, the Rensselaer Iron Works, the Bessemer Steel Works, and the Burden Iron Works. The first three firms later combined to form the Troy Iron and Steel Company. Total employment in all of the plants combined was about 2,500 people in 1880. These plants lit up the nighttime sky as they produced products vital to the growth of the United States, such as railroad track, valves, railroad spikes, axles, nuts, bolts, horseshoes, and chain. The Bessemer Steel Works produced the first steel in the United States on

February 16, 1865, in its plant near the mouth of the Wynantskill.

The Albany Iron Works, just up the hill from there, produced the rivets and metal plates for the ironclad ship *Monitor* in 1861. Although Troy's role as an iron-making center began to decline early in this century, other avenues were explored. Here is a view of the coke plant across from the Iron Works Station on the New York Central's beltline. Established in 1925 by the Burden Company, the plant was located on the site of the Bessemer Steel Plant. By 1938 it was using a half-million tons of coal per year to produce the coke and gas used by industrial and residential customers. Employing nearly 475 workers at its peak, it sold up to eighteen million cubic feet of gas daily, which was

stored in the huge metal tank which remains a landmark in South Troy today.

In the early 1960s the plant was no longer in use and was purchased by King Fuel, a heating oil and gasoline distributor. The company has adaptively reused many of the coke plant's structures. The newest commercial activity on this site is a distribution center for Coors Beer, being built by King Fuels and leased to Fitzgeralds, a local beverage distributor. The vast expanses of factories along the river are now gone, except for the lower mill of the Albany Iron Works, which is still being used by Portek, Inc., a company which produces high-tech insulated railroad track joints. *Courtesy of Rensselaer County Historical Society*

146

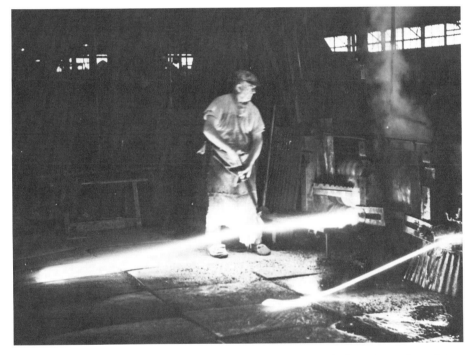

In a 1904 book about her father, Margaret Burden Proudfit described operations inside the Burden Iron Company Plant in South Troy. "The visitor beholds a scene of stirring activity seldom witnessed elsewhere. Scattered in groups or dispersed singly through this spacious building are hundreds of brawny men, with faces bedewed with perspiration and begrimed with coal dust, nude to their waists, their feet incased in heavy hob-nailed shoes, and their strong hands turning, thrusting, pulling, and piling the molten or fashioned iron in ways in- numerable amid the heat, the smoke and the short-lived splendor of a thousand red-hot metallic sparks."

In the 1930s, after the Burden Iron Company went into receivership, a number of former employees made an effort to run the plant as the Troy Furnace Corporation. Here is Pat Hines, in 1937, shaping bar iron in one of the Burden factories in the Lower Works, reminiscent of the workers some three decades earlier. *Courtesy of Rensselaer County Historical Society*

In 1862, the Burden Iron Company began to build a new plant on a forty-five-acre farm lying between the railroad and the river in South Troy. Families of Scottish, English, and Welsh mechanics settled in adjacent neighborhoods with Irish workers and their families. At its peak, the Burden Iron Company employed more than fourteen hundred men with an annual output of more than fifty million horseshoes.

Burden's son James possessed mechanical skills which improved the company's fortune, and in 1925 a new blast furnace was erected. The company flourished until the Great Depression, when it began to decline as part of a general slowdown of Troy's role as an iron-making center. In the modern age of steel and automobiles, with plant machinery tending toward obsolescence, less innovation, increasing labor demands, and the emergence of new steel companies in the West, the iron industry in Rensselaer County declined.

Republic Steel purchased the Works around 1940 and continued to produce high quality pig iron until the early 1970s. Virtually all of the structures in this circa 1910 view of the Burden Iron Works are gone today and the site is covered with rubble, weeds, and young trees. The ornate office building circa 1881-1882 (far right) is in the process of being restored by its present owners, the Hudson-Mohawk Industrial Gateway. *Courtesy of Hudson-Mohawk Industrial Gateway*

The textile and needle trades supported many thousands of Rensselaer County residents, principally women, from the mid-nineteenth to mid-twentieth centuries. Early in this century Cluett Peabody employed nearly six thousand people, including both workers at its Troy plant and the women throughout the county to whom they delivered piecework. Long before foreign competition loomed and obsolescence threatened, Cluett was called the largest manufacturer of its kind in the world.

Presently only corporate finance and data processing functions are carried out at Cluett's River Street plant, and the waterfront district which gave Troy its title of "Collar City" is now the scene of more diverse activities. Standard Manufacturing, specializing in outerwear, continues the textile tradition in its block-long Lion Shirt factory on Second Avenue, and Marvin-Neitzel still produces nurses' uniforms at their factory on River Street. *Courtesy of Rensselaer County Historical Society*

The lack of land in Albany for needed railroad facilities made the city of Rensselaer a logical location. The New York Central and the Boston and Albany railroads maintained large complexes for the servicing of locomotives and cars. Here is a New York Central J-3a Hudson and one of her sisters at their engine terminal in 1938. The locomotives, built in Schenectady, were styled by Henry Dreyfuss, a New York industrial designer, and used for the new edition of the Twentieth Century Limited. Both the Boston and Albany and New York Central facilities went into oblivion, as did the locomotives. Rensselaer High School now occupies this site. *Courtesy of Kalmbach Publishing Company*

In 1916, the Roebling family donated funds for the establishment of a radio station at RPI. (Washington Roebling, an RPI graduate, was chief engineer for the Brooklyn Bridge, designed by his father John.) It was not until World War I was over that the new station could be developed. Begun in 1922, WHAZ was the first college installed system for general broadcasting. The setup was through the Department of Electrical Engineering and was a pioneer in the early phase of commercial radio. Its general broadcast studio programs covered a worldwide area reaching Europe, Australia, and New Zealand. Another RPI station from the 1920s, 2SZ, is still on the air as RPI's amateur radio station, W2SZ. *Courtesy of Rensselaer County Historical Society*

Modernizing and rebuilding the movie houses to meet the times was the thing to do in the 1930s and 1940s. The Bijou, a neighborhood theater at Fifth Avenue and 112th Street in Troy, advertised the luxury of air conditioning along with the double feature in 1941. During the Second World War it was a regular ritual for those on the home front to try to get to a local movie house to see at least the *March of Time* or some other current picture newsreel from the battlefronts throughout the world. This visual news helped to supplement the radio broadcasts of news. *Courtesy of Rensselaer County Historical Society*

These students, physical education majors at Russell Sage College, are testing their strength! In 1930 the Central School of Physical Education from New York City became part of Russell Sage College and moved their staff to Troy. For many years, Sage was a leading school in training students to be physical education teachers. *Courtesy of Russell Sage College Archives*

Rensselaer County has two small airports, one at Castleton-on-Hudson and the County Airport at Poestenkill. Both serve small private planes. In the 1930s the Troy Airport, pictured here, was located near Campbell Avenue. Advertisements of the time called it "one of the finest fields for private fliers in the East...equipped with beacon, approach and obstruction lights." The ads also reassured fliers on a tight budget with the notation that there was "no charge for landing or floodlighting." The airport no longer exists and the land is now used for the Troy Industrial Park and Emerald Greens Homes. *Courtesy of Rensselaer County Historical Society*

During the 1930s people in the county and surrounding areas had two floating nightclubs which proved very popular. Prohibition had been repealed by the Twenty-First Amendment to the United States Constitution in December 1933, and dining and dancing establishments seemed to pop up everywhere after that, even though those were Depression years.

The *Ship of Joy,* a river barge converted into a nightclub in 1931, was moored in the Hudson River at 109th Street in the Lansingburgh area of Troy. Its interior had room for both dining and dancing, and it featured the well-known local group, the Charles Randall Dance Band. The barge was hit by a large section of floating ice in the spring freshets of 1935 and sank at its dock.

Another club, *The Paradise,* was located in a masted schooner moored in Troy at the foot of Fulton Street. This was an extremely large club with a dining room and large dance floor on the main deck, and a tap room and grill on the lower deck. *The Paradise* was grounded in the flood of 1936 and was later towed from Troy to Staten Island. *Courtesy of Frances D. Broderick*

Babcock Lake in the Grafton Mountains is named after an early settler, "Honest John" Babcock. It has been an active private resort since its development in 1925 by a Brooklyn corporation which built roads and introduced electric power and a water supply. There were cabins, a lodge, and many fine summer homes. The development changed ownership through the years and since 1975 the cottage and home owners, many of whom live there year-round, maintain their own association. This photo from 1941 shows the dock and bathing facilities. A car was necessary to get there since the lake was far from public transportation. *Courtesy of Rensselaer County Historical Society*

One of the great entertainment spots of the 1930s and early 1940s was the Club Edgewood at East Greenbush. A dance and supper club with the capacity for twelve hundred or more people, it brought to the area such famous dance bands as Frankie Carle, Blue Barron, Sammy Kaye, and Harry James. The club was destroyed by fire in the early morning of March 16, 1941. It was not rebuilt but the land became the site of the Mount Vernon Motel. The Mount Vernon, like other early motels, was considered extremely modern because it gave traveling motorists a place to park their cars directly outside their accommodations. *Glen Cook photo; courtesy of Leonard S. Schell*

Russell Sage College did its part to prepare its students to take over "men's work" should the United States enter World War II. An article in *Life* magazine for December 16, 1940, described the defense program and showed girls being trained to repair trucks, handle fire-fighting equipment and care for the wounded. Here a saddle-shoed student, Betty Tapley, practices her skills on a 1939 Pontiac. *Courtesy of Russell Sage Archives*

Once America had entered World War II, all Rensselaer County residents did what they could to help the war effort. These two women helped staff a booth at the Schaghticoke Fair, encouraging all who passed to buy war bonds. *Courtesy of Richard Lohnes*

Fireworks over the Hudson River and Troy were part of a celebration of Riverfront Park's first anniversary. *Luanne M. Ferris photo; courtesy of the* Times Record

Chapter Six

1946-1987
Working Toward Tomorrow

As the soldiers came home from World War II, the overwhelming impetus was a "return to normal." Returning veterans enrolled in local colleges under the GI Bill and bought homes with VA mortgages. The nuclear family in its own suburban house became the ideal, and new neighborhoods sprang up across the countryside. Sprawling town centers were further attenuated by upgraded highways and eventually by the interstate highways, which brought many more workers from the cities of Albany and Troy out to subdivisions on the former farmlands of Brunswick, Greenbush, Nassau, Schodack, and Schaghticoke.

Downtowns tried to fight back with urban renewal programs to remove deteriorated old buildings and create gracious new spaces. The results were not always immediately pleasing. Downtown Troy sat, half-decimated, for years before the Uncle Sam Atrium could be completed. Recent restoration activities and facade improvement grant programs have brought new life to Troy, Hoosick Falls, Rensselaer, Grafton and other communities and point to a vibrant future for the area.

In addition to population shifts, the county has also faced major shifts in its industrial base. As in all of America, manufacturing industries have declined while service industries have increased. Education has become a major industry in Rensselaer County, accounting for a substantial portion of the county's economy. New high-tech industries like those in North Greenbush's RPI Technology Park or in Poestenkill point the way to a new tax base.

As improved transportation and communication continue to reduce the barriers of time and distance, Rensselaer County's disparate towns have come to recognize their common needs and resources. In the years since World War II, individual city and town welfare and health departments have been consolidated into county-wide agencies. An active local campaign for a more responsible form of county government resulted in the 1970 replacement of the Board of Supervisors with an elected county legislature and an elected county executive. New comprehensive schools with fleets of buses anchor school districts which often transcend township lines.

The nation's bicentennial in 1976 and new economic incentives have refocused interest on the county's remarkable historic buildings, prompting new investment in the communities, restoration of old homes, and new businesses in once empty blocks. There is a new interest in local history as the county moves into its fourth century of settlement and approaches the bicentennial of its own political founding. Poised on the edge of the twenty-first century, Rensselaer County takes account of her past even as she turns toward the future.

Although Russell Sage was a college for women, in the postwar period (1946-50) it established a men's division to accommodate some of the veterans taking advantage of the GI Bill. For much of the time the men were instructed in separate classes and then the program was phased out and they transferred to other colleges. In May 1987 the trustees of Russell Sage reaffirmed their dedication to the college to continue its single-sex tradition, one of a small number of such institutions remaining. *Courtesy of Russell Sage College Archives*

In the early 1950s, downtown Troy's cast iron streetlight posts seemed outdated and were replaced by a new lighting system worthy of a primary business area. With an annual sales volume in excess of $110 million, Troy's business district had yet to feel the effects of suburban shopping centers. Here is a view of the new lighting on Broadway at Second Street looking east. Patrons of the Hendrick Hudson Hotel could stroll through the city or take in a show at Proctor's under the new "Westinghouse luminaries." *Courtesy of Rensselaer County Historical Society*

They were called the gridiron shows of the Troy Newswriters and they were highly successful. Leading area politicians came each year to see how the press would roast them. The two key men who brought these shows into being for thirty years (1933-1963) were John J. Givney, Sr., who wrote them, and Joseph J. Horan, who directed them. In the 1954 Gridiron Show, the cast included (from left) Joe Fitzgerald, John Dillon, Joseph A. Parker, William R. Browne, Jack Demers, and Daniel W. Costello. *Jack Short photo; courtesy of the* Times Record

Around the turn of the century, when Averill Park was the terminus of the Troy and New England Railway trolley, many good-sized hotels served vacationers who thronged to this town of seven lakes. Today people still drive to the village of Averill Park to enjoy the restaurant and inn at the Gregory House. Built in 1830 by Elias Gregory, this was the home of one of a large number of Gregorys who were active in Sand Lake's affairs from its earliest days. *Courtesy of Bette and Bob Jewell*

Farming is still an integral part of the lives of many residents in this county. In many towns, generations of a family have worked on the same farms through good times and bad. Farm children have a unique opportunity to participate in their parents' work, and organizations such as 4-H clubs assist in that association. Here the four Phillips children (Clark, Herbert, Forman, and Barbara Ellen) pose with their animals on their North Greenbush farm. *Courtesy of David Phillips*

It was in 1819 that the Rensselaer County Agricultural Society was formed and held its first fair on the riverbank south of Hoosick Street in Troy. Through the years with various societies and names, the fair has flourished. It has been held in Troy, Lansingburgh, West Sand Lake, and other places. In 1921 Schaghticoke was chosen as the permanent site with the fair to be held annually, usually around the Labor Day weekend. There are many exhibition buildings, a stadium and a racetrack.

An aerial photograph on Labor Day 1946 shows the crowds which turned out for the first peacetime fair gathering after World War II. *George Sample photo; courtesy of Schaghticoke Fair*

Agricultural fairs offer excitement as well as edification—"1000 Thrills," as a 1936 poster proclaimed. After you saw "Lucky" Teter hurtling over a large truck you might pitch baseballs at a moving target to win an orange bear, accompanied by calliope music amidst the squeals of delight emanating from mechanical swings and caterpillars. And of course you would see the best animals, the best jars of preserves, and the best 4-H projects. Fifty years after "Lucky" Teter, an avid multitude still looks forward to *this* year's Schaghticoke Fair. *Courtesy of Schaghticoke Town Historian*

For twenty years (1955-1975), sixty-five different species of exotic wild animals could be seen in the town of West Sand Lake. Fox's Game Farm, owned and operated by Harold Fox and his wife, attracted tourists and school groups from all over the region. In the last few years of its existence, over eighty thousand people a year came to the farm to look at the chimpanzee family, wildcats of all kinds, snow leopards, a baby elephant, and an eight-foot ostrich. Hoofed beasts such as antelopes and llamas roamed in corrals while more delicate or dangerous species such as lions or thousand-dollar monkeys were kept in cages. The Foxes also operated a zoo-mobile, taking about ten animals at a time around to every school in the Capital District. They had some assistance from Annette Schenker, a Swiss zoologist who lived in East Greenbush and was photographed holding these twenty-five-day-old lion cubs.

A game farm of exotic beasts was expensive to run, particularly with the big cats eating thirty to forty pounds of meat a day, but the final blow was Mr. Fox's health. After he had a heart attack in 1976, the family decided to close the farm, but it took another two years before they were able to find new homes in other zoos and game farms for the more than three hundred animals they owned. *Steven Lovelett photo; courtesy of the* Times Record

Located on White Lily Pond at Grafton, Camp Yowochas was a girls' YWCA summer camp of many years. A live-away camp providing sports of all kinds, it also had arts and crafts with excellent supervision by talented counselors. The costs of staffing, high cost of maintenance and prohibitive costs of insurance have caused the demise of many youth camps. In the 1970s this camp was purchased by the Troy Housing Authority, renamed Camp Hayes and became a day camp for some 250 children from the inner-city. It, too, is no longer operating because of the high cost of liability insurance. *Jack Short photo; courtesy of YWCA*

President Dwight Eisenhower conferred with Congressman Dean P. Taylor of Troy at the White House in 1956 when Eisenhower was elected to his second term. At the time, Taylor was committeeman of the National Republican Party. Taylor also was the Republican Party State Chairman and was influential in getting many public housing loans for Troy. As county chairman he made the designations for political jobs. Taylor was in Congress from 1943 to 1962. He was a friend of Governor Thomas E. Dewey, and Vice President Richard M. Nixon came to Troy in 1960 for a testimonial dinner for Taylor.

Other congressmen from Rensselaer County who have served in Washington were William D. Thomas of Hoosick Falls (1934-36), E. Harold Cluett of Troy (1936-42), and, in more recent years, Edward W. (Ned) Pattison of West Sand Lake (1975-78). *White House photo; courtesy of Mrs. Dean P. Taylor*

The Rutland Railroad's "Corkscrew Division" line to Chatham disappeared from the upper Taconic Valley in the spring of 1953, after eighty-three years of existence. Here the local freight to Rutland is shown crossing the Boston and Maine tracks at Petersburgh Junction during its last weeks of operation. It has just come north through the Little Hoosic River Valley.

Today the Rutland is only a memory, its roadbed plowed under by farmers. The station is gone, the B & M track abandoned. *Jim Shaughnessy photo; courtesy of the photographer*

Rensselaer County native Jim Shaughnessy, a widely recognized railroad photographer and author, takes us back in time with this scene of Troy Union Station, looking south about 1954. Delaware and Hudson No. 34, the Laurentian, has just arrived from Montreal and the station has come to life. Employees move about in the chilled air, pedestrians watch, and the baggage cart is eased toward the train along Fulton Street. The train will soon continue on its way to New York City and passengers inside the warm stainless steel observation car (foreground) will watch the city go by, passing on the left a coal car near the depot steam plant, and across Broadway, the Lowe funeral coach rental business and an abandoned shirt factory. On the right the train will pass Pat Clarey's restaurant, Mame Fay's red-light district, and the adjacent police station. The train will then pass through the Congress/Ferry Street tunnel, ease across the streets near Washington Park, and then race to Grand Central Terminal. *Jim Shaughnessy photo; courtesy of the photographer*

Milk was an important county product, and the rail network provided a convenient connection with Boston and New York metropolitan markets. Here is the daily Delaware and Hudson milk train in 1959, with a classic Borden glass-insulated milk car. Leaving Green Island each morning, the train traversed a route through Troy to Eagle Bridge (the location of a Hood Plant which shipped to Boston), crossed over the Hoosic River to Rutland, and then returned to Green Island via Whitehall, picking up milk and returning empties. A locomotive from Troy's Adams Street Yard then picked up the cars for transport to New York City.

Milk trains became a thing of the past when the New England states, Vermont in particular, were cut out of the New York City milkshed by federal decree in the late 1950s. *Jim Shaughnessy photo; courtesy of the photographer*

The Boston and Maine bridge across the Hudson River in northern Rensselaer County stands as tangible evidence of a dream to build a railroad from the Hoosac Tunnel to Oswego and Buffalo to compete with the powerful New York Central Railroad. In 1879 the Boston, Hoosac Tunnel and Western was built parallel to the Troy and Boston across the county to Johnsonville, where the line veered west to cross the Hudson above Mechanicville, going as far as Rotterdam Junction on the Mohawk River where it connected with West Shore Railroad, a New York City competitor at that time. From Eagle Bridge to Schaghticoke the line utilized the abandoned roadbed of the old Albany Northern. In Hoosick Falls a two-story station was built where the Boston, Hoosac Tunnel and Western and the Troy and Boston crossed each other on different levels. Both lines became the Fitchburg, and then in 1900 the Boston and Maine. The Boston and Maine continued to use both lines, which posed a problem for Buskirk passengers. Timetables stated: "East Buskirk and Buskirk stations are in the same town, about one-half mile apart; passengers westbound take trains at East Buskirk, eastbound at Buskirk." Guilford Lines now operates trains over the old Boston and Maine route. *Jim Shaughnessy photo; courtesy of the photographer*

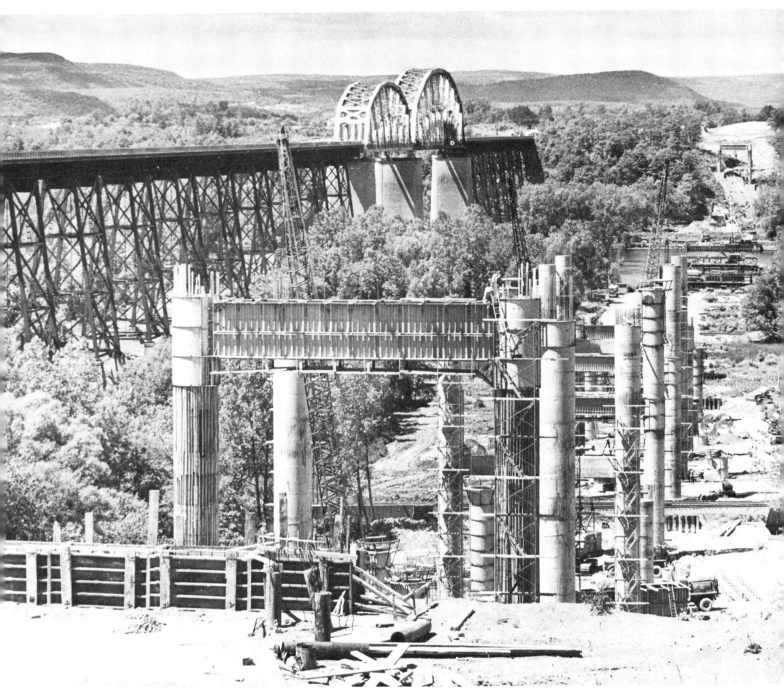

In 1957 the Berkshire Spur of the New York State Thruway was under construction. Crossing Rensselaer and Columbia counties to connect the Thruway at Selkirk with the Massachusetts Turnpike twenty-five miles to the south, it was a major link in the interstate network from Boston to Chicago until the completion of I-90 through Albany.

The new spur crossed the Hudson River next to the main line of the New York Central Railroad and soon took much of the railway's freight and passenger business. In an effort to compete with the highways, the New York Central would merge with its old archenemy, the Pennsylvania, to become the Penn Central in 1968, but the new line sank into bankruptcy only seven years later. It was reborn as Conrail in 1976 and has become a profitable carrier once again. *Courtesy of Capital Newspapers*

In 1942 the Veterans Vocational School was established for defense and war training. It was housed in the vacant Earl Wilson shirt factory, a seven-story building on Seventh Avenue at Broadway in Troy. A small supplemental building was used on Bond Street. By 1950, thirteen trades and skills were taught in twenty-one shops and laboratories and as many classrooms. When the State Education Department discontinued the school in 1953, a group of citizens led by Dwight Marvin, editor for The Record Newspapers, petitioned the Board of Supervisors to sponsor an institute to replace the vocational school. This was done and in September 1953 a two-year college officially opened with eighty-eight students. The next year assets were transferred from state to county operation.

Five years later, some Rensselaer County citizens brought suit to end county financing of the college because students from outside the county were attending. The court's verdict favored county support. The following year, ground was broken for a modern campus in North Greenbush completed in 1960. The school, renamed Hudson Valley Community College, now has full transfer credit to the State University of New York system. Many students also transfer to other colleges after completing their two-year program here. Recent programs have been expanded beyond the first largely technical ones to include health sciences, business and liberal arts.
Courtesy of Hudson Valley Community College Media Center

A thunderous explosion shook the hamlet of Berlin late in the afternoon of July 25, 1962. It was caused by the crash of a propane gas truck which went out of control on the downgrade of Plank Road on the western side of the village. The truck's driver, Robert J. McLucas, of Pomeroy, Pennsylvania and nine residents of the village died as a result of the fire. Sixteen persons were injured and many buildings were set on fire, including the First Baptist Church. This is a previously unpublished photograph showing what happened to two school buses parked in a nearby garage.
Courtesy of Katherine Wells

An aerial view of Carroll's Hill shows the expansion within Troy's city limits after World War II. The large buildings of Griswold Heights, a state financed low-income housing project built in the 1950s, are on the site of the old Rensselaer County Welfare Home. In front of them, the subdivision of private homes called Hillsview Heights, completed in the late 1960s, and the private apartment complex, Riverview Apartments, were built on the site of Troy's first airport (1920-27). To accommodate the many children of all the new housing, the Carroll Hill Elementary School was constructed in the mid-sixties. *Al Livingstone photo; courtesy of the* Times Record

Schaghticoke, Troy, North Greenbush, and Brunswick began to study their municipal sewage treatment problems in 1963, under a Public Health Service grant. At that time practically all sewage and industrial waste in the Capital District were discharged raw into the Hudson River. By 1969 Rensselaer County Sewer District No. 1 was created, including the above municipalities plus the city of Rensselaer and a portion of Sand Lake. With several municipalities involved, a strong leader was needed. That person was Commission Chairman Richard Keeler, county legislator and supervisor, at the time, of Brunswick. Keeler brought together all the parties involved and coordinated the process with the State. Commission negotiations included the significant financial role of four Rensselaer industries which would be major contributors to the system: Sterling Organics, Sterling Winthrop Research Institute, GAF (now BASF) and Huyck Mills (the latter has since closed). Engineering design was by Malcolm Pirnie, Inc. Construction began at the site on the banks of the Hudson River, one mile south of Menands Bridge, in 1973. In 1976 the plant began operating, thus allowing cleanup of the Hudson River where it borders Rensselaer County, aided now by new sewage treatment plants at East Greenbush and Castleton-on-Hudson. *Courtesy of Rensselaer County Sewer District No. 1*

In 1966, Troy completed a rejuvenation of its water system, including a new treatment plant, larger water mains and three storage tanks. The tank from which this photograph was taken is located on Tibbetts Avenue, at the highest point in the city to provide proper water pressure. Robert Merithew was inspecting the tank interior at the time. To the left may be seen part of RPI's Linear Accelerator and the RPI Field House. *Michael McMahon photo; courtesy of the* Times Record

The Fox Hollow Festival of traditional music and arts was presented annually by the Beers family on their estate on Route 2, west of Petersburg, from 1965 to 1980. The four day summer festival with performances on a stage in an outdoor amphitheater brought sound in a natural setting to the audiences. Thousands attended each year to hear well-known artists of recording and stage fame, family singing groups and national/regional performers. They sang and played old ballads, ditties, riddle songs, and songs for many kinds of dancing and activities, using traditional instruments. The festival featured arts and crafts, as well as time for folks to get acquainted with performers and one another. The festivals were an outstanding contribution to the study and development of folk music and crafts in this country. *Courtesy of Evelyne Beers Burnstine*

The RPI Engineers' Hockey Team is the main attraction when they play at their home base in the Houston Field House at Rensselaer Polytechnic Institute in Troy. The Field House is an outstanding facility for recreation and entertainment in Rensselaer County. It hosts more than a hundred events a year among which are rodeos, exhibitions, circuses, concerts and the annual visit of the National Ice Capades. The rink is open for public skating and is used by colleges, high schools, and various junior hockey clubs for practice and games. It is well known to area parents as the home of peewee hockey. *Courtesy of Rensselaer Polytechnic Institute*

Through the years circuses and carnivals have played the county seat. They gathered under the big top at Groveland Track near Rensselaer Park, and in later years under the roof of the RPI Field House. Here is a line of eighteen elephants from the Ringling Brothers Barnum and Bailey Circus making their way to the Field House which was packed for all of their performances May 25-30, 1986. In earlier years the shows arrived on colorful circus trains but today trailers, caravans and large trucks are employed to move the circuses, carnivals and traveling shows on their seasonal tours. Although the romance of a full circus parade may have disappeared, the sight of elephants marching through the streets of Troy had the power to create magical memories for these children.
Courtesy of Rensselaer County Historical Society

East Greenbush's busiest corner is Route 9 and 20 (Columbia Turnpike) and Route 4 (Troy Road). Workmen are shown resurfacing Columbia Turnpike in 1978. Behind the workers can be seen some of the modern strip development which has sprung up along the highway. Unlike downtown blocks built in the days of horses and pedestrians, these buildings are designed to catch the eye of customers zipping past in their cars. The large signs can be easily seen from a great distance and the lots are arranged to provide ample room for the omnipresent automobile. As the car continues to dominate local transportation, developments such as this can be found in every township of the county.
Michael McMahon photo; courtesy of the Times Record

The construction of interstate highway systems has dramatically altered the landscape of our countryside as well as our perception of time and distance. The completion of I-90 across Rensselaer County brought much of East Greenbush, Schodack, and Nassau into commuting distance for workers in Albany and Troy, while I-787 and the new Route 7, both in Albany County, have bound the communities of the Capital District even closer together. Looking toward Rensselaer County from the massive four-level Patroon Island interchange, I-90 crosses the Hudson River on a twelve million dollar bridge, opened in 1969. Seven years later the highway was completed down through the county to the Berkshire Spur, creating development along its route, particularly at the Route 4 interchange in recent years. *Courtesy of Capital Newspapers*

Debris covered the ground as the Green Island bridge was hurriedly dismantled in April 1977, following its collapse during high flood waters on March 15. A new $22.1 million lift-bridge opened in 1981 on new piers, replacing the old ones which had been the cause of the collapse.

Bridges have crossed the Hudson here since 1835, when the Rensselaer and Saratoga built a long wooden bridge with a swing span. When the new Troy Union Station was opened in 1854, the bridge was enlarged to accommodate locomotives. It was on this bridge that sparks from a locomotive started the disastrous fire of 1862. Several spans followed and during the construction of the Champlain Barge Canal in 1915, a lift span was added on the Troy side. Trains vanished from the bridge in 1963, and the north side was converted for auto use. *G. Steven Draper photo; courtesy of the photographer*

Throughout the county in 1976, citizens celebrated the bicentennial of America's founding with parades, festivals, and special reenactments. Patriotic symbols were painted on buildings and fire hydrants, while red, white, and blue became the most prominent colors in sight.

Rensselaer warmed up for these activities with festivities in 1975 celebrating the bicentennial of the Fort Crailo charter. Watched over by Uncle Sam (Tom Greeley of Troy), East Greenbush Town Supervisor Michael Van Voris (left) and Rensselaer Mayor Joseph Mink (right) reenacted the signing of the charter which years ago settled a dispute over the ownership of Fort Crailo. *C. W. McKeen photo; courtesy of the* Times Record

Wynantskill Fire Department officials in 1978 displayed an old fire truck with a new fire rescue truck. From left are: Richard Brimmer, captain; Robert Miller, president; James Burt, custodian; Louis Capano, lieutenant; William Gummer, chief, and James Oliver, assistant chief. In recent years fire departments in the county have added paramedic services to their list of skills. A certification program has been added and all personnel have training in life-rescue techniques. *D. Gross photo; courtesy of the* Times Record

The new three-story Troy City Hall was completed in 1974 after a long wait. The old city hall burned in 1938 and it was felt that Troy could not afford a new structure because of the large amount of tax-exempt property in the city. Finally in 1972 John P. Buckley, city manager, and the Democratic City Council decided that with the help of federal revenue sharing funds, Troy could have a new building. Designed by the Troy architectural firm of Cadman, Droste and Thomas, the completely furnished building cost a total of $2.8 million. Seventy percent of its superstructure is made of precast concrete sections. The building faces Monument Square while large window areas in the rear provide interesting views of Riverfront Park and the Hudson. *Terry G. Weaver photo; courtesy of Troy City Hall*

John P. Buckley (left), Troy's fifth city manager, was the first to make the manager system work successfully. He still had problems working with the city council, and he was fired in 1977. He was returned to office the following year, however, and served well until his retirement in June 1986. Before becoming city manager, Buckley overhauled Troy's Water Department and directed the building of the new filtration plant and the replacement of city water lines. He set up an excellent water supply system to provide for the city and for its sale to nearby communities. He is pictured here with George O'Connor, public safety commissioner. *Courtesy of the* Times Record

Edward F. McDonough was elected chairman of the Rensselaer County Democratic Committee in 1968 when there were few Democrats holding county posts. He has held the post longer than any Democratic Party chairman. In quiet, behind-the-scenes action, he has directed the party election campaigns to give the Democrats the edge over the Republicans in county and Troy governments. *Courtesy of the* Times Record

In an effort to bring new life into depressed cities and to help downtown shops compete with new suburban shopping centers, the federal and state governments instituted urban renewal grant programs in the late 1960s. The Troy Urban Renewal Agency was created by the state legislature in 1966; they began demolishing hundreds of old buildings soon thereafter and offered the cleared land for new construction. It wasn't until the late 1970s that old buildings came back into favor and restoration became an option once again.

The Urban Renewal Agency's biggest project was the purchase in 1972 of 122 downtown properties in the area of the Troy/Green Island bridge for almost ten million dollars. Sixty-three buildings were leveled by work crews to make room for the Uncle Sam Mall and for street realignment and widening. The land was quickly cleared, but the mall experienced lengthy delays before it could be built. *C. W. McKeen photo; courtesy of the* Times Record

Another facet of the Urban Renewal Program was the creation of new housing units. Entire blocks of small brick rowhouses like these desolate survivors were torn down and modern highrises like the Kennedy Towers rose in their place. Completed in 1967, the tower was named for the late president and cost $4.25 million to build. Its twenty-one-story precast concrete walls enclose apartments for senior citizens. Fifteen senior citizens housing complexes provide services for seniors throughout the county. A second housing project, Troy Towers for middle-income families, and the Holiday Inn now stand on the cleared land in the photo. *Jim Shaughnessy photo; courtesy of the* Troy Record

Bright street lights lend splendor to this night scene of Troy's changing downtown in 1977. The small lake in the foreground is now the location of Troy Parking Garage. Frear's is on the left. At right the lighted building is the Peerless Company store at River and Fulton; on its right was Denby's. Peerless's building was torn down shortly after this photo was taken and Peerless moved to the Frear Building. Denby's moved into the Uncle Sam Atrium in the fall of 1978. *Courtesy of the* Times Record

It was a busy day after Thanksgiving in 1980 when shoppers converged on the Troy Atrium to see the holiday decorations and begin their Christmas shopping. They were a welcome sight to merchants who had watched acres of downtown remain empty for almost four years. Carl Grimm, a native of Troy and an RPI graduate, got things moving again when he was able to buy the land bounded by Fulton, Fourth, Broadway, and Third streets. He then constructed a two-story mall, naming it the Uncle Sam Atrium, which first opened in November 1978. The Troy Parking Garage was built simultaneously, and the two structures have convenient connections between them. *Thomas Killips photo: courtesy of the Troy Record*

Russell Sage College quickly outgrew its nucleus of buildings from the original Emma Willard School, and it adapted adjoining downtown brownstones for dormitories and dining rooms. All of the structures in the block of Second Street between Division and Ferry streets were torn down in the 1950s to make room for the James Wheelock Library and the Science Building.

In the 1960s, when a proposed widening of Ferry Street threatened to destroy the campus, President Lewis Froman initiated a move to build a tunnel for the road from River Street to Third Street. This was completed in the early 1970s and in 1983 the ground above was dedicated as the Froman Mall. Adjacent to it an area previously occupied by college buildings was transformed into the Schacht Gardens, given by Elmer Schacht in memory of his wife. *Jim Shaughnessy photo; courtesy of Russell Sage Archives*

The intersection of Route 4 and Hoosick Street in Troy shows the dramatic changes which took place there between 1934 and 1980. Buses had just taken over from the trolleys in 1934 and the tracks had been covered. Many of the buildings pictured in the earlier photo were torn down to make room for a shopping center. The greatest change, however, was in the road itself which split into two levels to separate local river-front traffic from those cars traveling across the river toward Latham on the new Route 7. *Courtesy of Keith Marvin and Rensselaer County Historical Society*

The Turkey Trot is an appropriate name for a morning race on Thanksgiving Day in Troy. The run has been taking place since 1964 and is a continuation of the Troy Marathon which began in the early twentieth century. Hundreds of men, women, boys, and girls race in all different classes representing not only all corners of the county but also other states and foreign countries. With the increased popularity of jogging and running as a regular activity, the registration seems to increase each year. Because one cannot depend on the weather in November, the race has taken place in rain, snow, sleet, fog, and occasionally on a warm, sunny morning. *C. W. McKeen photo; courtesy of the* Times Record

Dwight Marvin, editor of The Record Newspapers, retired in 1959 after fifty-one years of service. He distinguished himself not only in his profession, but also as a community leader and a watchdog for good government. He was president of Troy Chromatics, on the board of trustees of Emma Willard School and the State University, chairman of the board of Hudson Valley Community College, and officer of many other organizations over the years. He was president of the American Society of Newspaper Editors during the 1930s. He is pictured at his desk at the time of his fiftieth anniversary with the paper in 1957. He was succeeded as editor by Alton T. Sliter, who was later editor and publisher until his retirement in 1972. Editors who followed were Joseph R. Snyder, Joseph A. Cooley, and Roland E. Blais. *William Coonley photo; courtesy of the* Times Record

State Assemblyman Neil W. Kelleher (left) and State Senator Joseph L. Bruno call out Bingo numbers in a photo taken at a Brunswick seniors' party. Kelleher, a former Troy mayor, has been serving as a Republican assemblyman since 1967. Senator Bruno, a Republican from Brunswick, has concentrated his efforts on invigorating business growth in the state and on consumer protection issues. As chairman of the Committee on Consumer Protection, he was successful in getting the car "lemon law" passed, as well as a law to discourage false advertising and deceptive business practices. *Luanne M. Ferris photo; courtesy of the* Times Record

The Rensselaer County Council for the Arts is housed in the former Uri Gilbert House on Troy's Washington Park, which is one of the last remaining private parks in the country. The Council was founded in 1962 to serve arts and cultural agencies and artists in the Rensselaer County area. It publishes an arts calendar, mounts art exhibits often featuring contemporary artists, and provides art courses of all kinds. In 1962 the RCCA began its annual Arts Festival which was presented in the park and showcased arts and crafts from a wide area. Twenty-one years later the festival moved to Riverfront Park where it attracts hundreds of people each year in one of the area's largest summer events. *Courtesy of Rensselaer County Council for the Arts*

To bring a more responsible government into the county a campaign was begun in 1969 by the Greater Troy Chamber of Commerce, The Record Newspapers, the County League of Women Voters, and other groups. Alton T. Sliter, editor of The Record Newspapers, was chosen chairman of the commission to draft a new charter for the county. The Board of Supervisors was replaced by the County Legislature in 1970. The following year the proposed charter was defeated by voters because it was felt that the new county executive should be elected rather than appointed. In 1972 a revised charter calling for an elected county executive met approval and in 1973 the Republican candidate, William J. Murphy of Hoosick Falls, was elected as the first county executive. He was re-elected in 1977 and 1981. In 1979 he was president of the National Association of the Counties. *Courtesy of the* Times Record

Rensselaer County residents take full advantage of the winter's snow and cold to enjoy sports and outdoor activities such as skating, sledding, downhill and cross-country skiing, as well as snowmobiling. Some of the many parks in the county which provide winter activities are Grafton Lake State Park, Dyken Pond Environmental Center, North Greenbush Town Park, Schermerhorn Park in Castleton-on-Hudson, and Frear Park in Troy. There are also commercial resorts for winter sports and some town roads are designated and posted for snowmobile use. This young man, Peter Elie, is enjoying a sled ride on a hill in Frear Park in February 1987. *Michael McMahon photo; courtesy of the* Times Record

From the time of its formal dedication with a great orchestra concert under Theodore Thomas on April 19, 1875, the Troy Savings Bank Music Hall has served as a center of cultural activity for the area. The hall, which seats twelve hundred people, is located on the floors above the bank, and some of the world's most renowned musical artists and orchestras have claimed that its acoustics are among the finest in the world. In the past the Music Hall served as home for the Troy Vocal Society and the Musical Arts Society. The Chromatic Concerts, now in their ninety-first season, have had all of their professional music series in the hall since 1918. For many years the hall has hosted numerous popular and classical concerts from September through May, as well as eight symphony concerts given by the Albany Symphony Orchestra, one of which is pictured here. *Stanley Blanchard photo; courtesy of Troy Liveability*

During some summer weeks more than three thousand people visit Grafton Lakes State Park in the town of Grafton. There are five lakes in the 2,000-acre park which were formerly part of the water supply for Troy. Long Lake has a great bathing beach and all facilities. Year-round the park offers hiking and nature trails as well as fishing. Boating is allowed on all lakes in summer and, in winter, ice skating, cross-country skiing, and snow-mobiling are also available. Not too many miles south of Grafton in Stephentown and Berlin is the 250-acre Cherry Plain State Park located on Black River Pond. Among its facilities are a beach, bathhouse, picnic tables, hiking trails, and a playground. That park is a former Civilian Conservation Corps (CCC) site of the 1930s. *Thomas Killips photo; courtesy of the* Times Record

In 1980 Sugi and Keith Picard, Annette Nanes, and Scott Meyer began the Third Street Theatre in the city of Rensselaer. The first of its kind in the area, the small theater offered moviegoers a selection of American independent and foreign films and soon developed a loyal audience. Moviegoers at Third Street were treated to pre-curtain slide shows, and could view regular features such as *Eraserhead* or *Polyester* while eating chocolate cake and drinking hot cider. Here in 1981 a group is settling in for a 3-D double feature—*Creature from the Black Lagoon* and *It Came From Outer Space.* In 1983, following increased patronage at their Third Street location, the owners renovated an old theater building in Albany, modifying it to make two viewing areas. Another screen was added there in January 1987, and the Rensselaer theater was closed to further consolidate operations. The homey charm of the original Third Street Theatre continues at the current Albany location. *Louise Kraznowitz photo; courtesy of Spectrum Theatres*

Founded in 1954 and now housed in the former J. J. Child Steam Fire Engine Company Building at 106th Street and Fifth Avenue, the Rensselaer County Junior Museum provides hands-on museum experience for children up to sixth grade. Providing concrete learning experiences in the natural sciences, it also offers a living history program called "Rich Folk—Poor Folk" in cooperation with the Rensselaer County Historical Society. *Courtesy of Rensselaer County Junior Museum*

Rensselaer County has had a fair share of state judges from among its many lawyers because of its proximity to the state capital. The Hon. A. Franklin Mahoney is currently presiding justice of the Appellate Division of the New York State Supreme Court, Third Judicial District. Other Troy lawyers who became justices of the Appellate Division were the Hon. John T. Casey, who is presently serving a term on the bench, and the late Hon. Donald S. Taylor. *Thomas Killips photo; courtesy of the* Times Record

For its 180th birthday in 1987, Grafton held a three-day celebration with parades and festivities for all ages. This picture shows a happy crowd enjoying a puppet show next to the bandstand in the town park; beyond that a line of people wait to be served a chicken barbecue in the churchyard. All fourteen townships in Rensselaer County are well over one hundred years old with Pittstown being the oldest, dating from 1761. *Thomas Killips photo; courtesy of the* Times Record

The city of Rensselaer's history has been intertwined with that of the railroad since 1841, when the first tracks reached the city from Massachusetts. Over the years, the yards, roundhouse, and other facilities needed to service engines and cars for the Boston and Albany and New York Central railroads became disused and eventually abandoned. Passenger service in New York State reached its lowest ebb on the eve of Amtrak taking over operation of all United States intercity passenger trains. In 1969 Penn Central, despite much protest, vacated Albany Union Station and constructed a new station in Rensselaer. At the time the local newspapers compared the new building's appearance with that of the local highway department's garages.

Ironically, the new structure was converted into a storage facility and offices only eleven years later when the present two million dollar glass and brick station was opened. With improved tracks, bridges, new locomotives and cars, and new Turboline trains, ridership has steadily increased. The railroad is often at its best in difficult weather, when other forms of transportation grind to a standstill. On a snowy morning in Feburary 1983, the Lake Shore Limited arrived at the depot from Chicago, encrusted with snow and ice. While passengers waiting to board remained in the comfort of the station, the train was divided into two trains; one went on to Boston, the other to Grand Central Terminal in New York City. *G. Steven Draper photo; courtesy of the photographer*

Raymond Foster began his career in 1887 as an errand boy for Schiefflin and Company, American agents for Bayer aspirin, which was a product of Frederick Bayer and Company of Germany. In 1904 the German chemical company diversified and began manufacturing Bayer aspirin in Rensselaer. Foster became president of The Bayer Company, Inc., and the facility came to be known locally as "the Bayer plant." When Foster retired in 1933 he was still an official in the company, which had been purchased in 1918 by Sterling Products Company (now Sterling Drug Inc.). In the ensuing years, Sterling's presence in Rensselaer County has grown to encompass three facilities: a modern manufacturing plant in East Greenbush, which produces prescription and over-the-counter medicines for the company's Pharmaceutical Group; the Sterling Organics plant in Rensselaer, which produces specialty chemicals and pharmaceutical intermediates; and the Sterling-Winthrop Research Institute, the company's primary research facility. In addition to Bayer aspirin, Sterling's products include Phillip's Milk of Magnesia, Panadol and Midol pain relievers, the Lysol brand line of household cleaner-disinfectants and many other medicines and household and consumer products. Sterling Drug Inc. is a multinational Fortune 250 company headquartered in New York City with operations in more than 125 countries and annual sales approximating two billion dollars. *Courtesy of Sterling Drug Inc.*

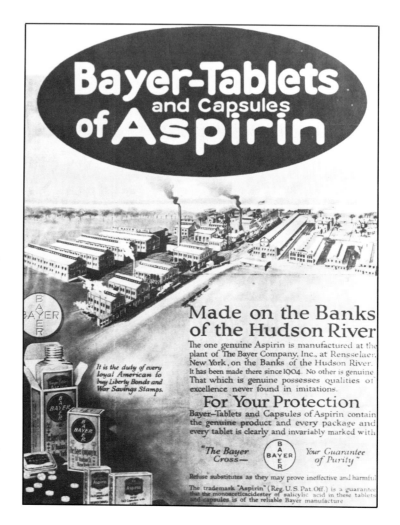

In 1986, when Congress declared the rose our national flower, Nancy Reagan's armful of blossoms from the Seagroatt Company in Berlin were part of the five million stems that Seagroatt markets each year. Seagroatt roses leave the greenhouse by truck and continue their journeys by land or air throughout the Northeast. Seven acres of glass, including a dozen new greenhouses, cover about 177,000 rose plants.

Henry J. Seagroatt was a florist in Berlin when he built his first greenhouse to grow roses in 1927. The family-run business has expanded; it now employs almost a hundred people and has a sister firm, a wholesale floral distributorship in Albany. *Hughes Gemmill photo; courtesy of the photographer*

Willis Judson Cowee was a sawmill operator in Berlin when he first noticed in a flower shop the small picks to which florists attached wire for securing floral displays. Inspiration struck young Cowee, and he began experimenting with a machine to attach wire to the pick. In 1900 he started the W. J. Cowee Company on the second floor of his sawmill, with the assistance of Peter Yerton. Other wood products were added to the line and the business expanded, moving into John Hewitt's wagon and bicycle shop, then to the old Earl and Wilson shirt factory, and finally to its present site.

Today Cowee's is the main industry in the town, employing about 150 people and managing thousands of acres of woodlands in New York, Vermont, and Massachusetts. They produce florists' picks, plant stakes, and custom turnings for toy manufacturers, such as yo-yo parts, beads, rings, and knobs. Before Tinker Toys began to be made from plastic, Cowee's made them from wood. Waste from the wood turnings is used to make steam, which in turn operates the electrical generators that power the factory. Surplus electricity is sold to the New York State Electric and Gas Company. *Courtesy of Berlin Town Historian*

BASF Wyandotte Corporation, a manufacturer of industrial dyes, has a plant at 36 Riverside Avenue in Rensselaer. It is one of the city's major employers, providing about five hundred jobs. The plant was purchased from GAF Corporation (originally General Aniline and Film Corporation). In 1986 the company paid more than $327,000 in city and school taxes. *Courtesy of the* Times Record

Musa, a London freight ship, unloads at the Port of Rensselaer, across from the Port of Albany. More ships are using the docking facilities on the Rensselaer County side and efforts are being made to enlarge the facility. Currently thirty-two feet deep and four hundred feet wide, the Port of Rensselaer handles 750,000 tons of cargo and 9 million tons of petroleum products annually. The major products which pass through these wharves are grain (wheat and corn), bananas, molasses, scrap iron, and motor vehicles. *Courtesy of the* Times Record

Norplex-Oak, a unit of Allied Signal Company, manufactures copper-clad laminates for the electronics industry in a plant constructed in 1981 on the site of the old Walter A. Wood complex. Allied Signal's three sites in Hoosick Falls employ a total of 550 people. Another unit which manufactures copper foil is located on the old Noble and Wood site, where equipment was once made for paper manufacturers. *G. Steven Draper photo; courtesy of the photographer*

County government expanded quickly after World War II as town and city welfare and health departments were consolidated into new county departments. The current Rensselaer County Office Building on Seventh Avenue in Troy was opened in 1978 and dedicated the following year. Many residents remember the building as the Troy High School, which was used from 1917 to the spring of 1952. In the fall of that year it became School No. 5 and continued as such into the 1970s. After classes were moved elsewhere, the former school was successfully renovated for county offices at a cost of $3.75 million. *Courtesy of Rensselaer County Public Affairs Office*

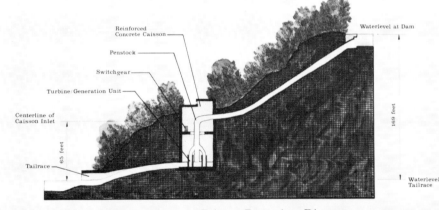

Caisson Powerplant Diagram

The potential of the Poestenkill Gorge's waterpower is being realized again with electricity generated by an innovative hydropower plant at the bottom of a pit that is ninety-four feet deep. For over three hundred years the Poestenkill Gorge had a succession of mills powered directly by water as the falls were channeled into conduits supplying a series of mills. The last of these mills, Manning Paper, moved its operations in 1962. After a twenty-one year hiatus, the Poesten-kill is again producing power at a rate even greater than what was considered possible just a few years ago.

The Mount Ida Hydroelectric Facility uses six hundred feet of Benjamin Marshall's original rock tunnel to divert water into its two spiral generators. Most of the power plant equipment is located in the forty-feet-diameter shaft pictured. *Courtesy of Mercer Companies, Inc.*

A new city charter instituting the city manager form of government went into effect on January 1, 1964, and Robert Stierer became Troy's first city manager. Steven G. Dworsky, shown here with John Buono, the county's second elected executive, is a former mayor of Troy who left his job as professor at HVCC to become the city's sixth manager, following a succession which included Sidney S. Smith, Adrian Gonyea, Ralph A. De Santes, and John Buckley. These men were all full-time administrators who succeeded the professional part-time politicians who once ran city and county affairs. *Courtesy of the* Times Record

Rensselaer County's Catholic and Episcopal churches serve a major portion of the county's population. In 1987 the Most Rev. Howard J. Hubbard (left), bishop of the Catholic Diocese of Albany, and the Right Rev. David S. Ball, bishop of the Episcopal Diocese of Albany, signed a historical ecumenical covenant between the two cathedrals of the dioceses. Local churches of these denominations look to the cathedrals in Albany as their "mother churches." Bishop Hubbard is the first head of the Albany Catholic Diocese to come from Rensselaer County. *Luanne M. Ferris photo; courtesy of the* Times Record

Farming in Rensselaer County has declined over the years as smaller farms have been absorbed into the larger operations. However, rural scenes such as this one in Stephentown in 1961 still abound. *Gene Baxter photo; courtesy of the* Times Record

Moon's Hotel at Barbersville Falls in Poestenkill is a very old landmark, located on Plank Road at the intersection of Columbia Hill Road below the Snake Hill cliffs. Henry Moon was the operator of the hotel in the 1870s. He was preceded by Isaac Allen, Wait Winchell, Burr Van Everen, Mr. Maxon, James Manning, and Benjamin Barber. The building is still standing and is now used for apartments. *Kathe Forster photo; courtesy of the* Times Record

In 1974 New York State voters approved the $250 million Rail Preservation Bond Act, which launched a track and station improvement program to implement high speed rail passenger service in the New York/Albany/Buffalo corridor. Of direct benefit to Rensselaer County was construction of a $15 million maintenance facility at Rensselaer, on the site of the old Boston and Albany Railroad servicing area, demolished many years earlier. The facility opened in 1976 and services the seven Rohr Turboliners, delivered that same year at a cost of $4.5 million each. Capable of speeds of up to 110 miles per hour, they are powered by gas turbines, and also feed off the electrified third rail between Harmon and Grand Central Terminal. The repair facility and station in Rensselaer employ close to three hundred people. This photo was taken on March 16, 1978. *Jim Shaughnessy photo; courtesy of the photographer*

Mass transportation has existed in Rensselaer County since the first horsecars were introduced prior to the Civil War. Created by the New York State Legislature in 1970, the Capital District Transportation Authority (CDTA) assumed operation of the former Albany-Nassau, Albany-Castleton, Troy Fifth Avenue, and United Traction bus companies within two years. In February 1981, CDTA dedicated the Troy facility near the Collar City Bridge which contains a bus wash, repair facility, dispatching unit, service area, and storage space for seventy buses. CDTA operates summer service to Grafton Lakes State Park, as well as the Schaghticoke Fair, and since 1982 has provided its Star service for disabled passengers. In 1984, the new Orion buses, built in Oriskany, New York, began replacing the older style Flxible's. CDTA also operates seven sixty-foot Crown-Ikarus articulated buses, built in Los Angeles. *G. Steven Draper photo; courtesy of the photographer*

Dedicated on May 14, 1987, the George M. Low Center for Industrial Innovation (CII) is Rensselaer Polytechnic Institute's newest campus structure and exemplifies the ties the college has had with American industry since its founding in 1824. The sixty million dollar nine-story building contains laboratories, offices, meeting rooms, a high bay area, and one of the largest clean rooms at any university in the East. The clean room is a virtually dust-free environment necessary for manufacturing tiny transmitters used in the semiconductor industry. The building is the result of a government, industry, and college partnership coordinated by George M. Low, RPI's fourteenth president and former NASA director. The building provides research space for many of the area's growing number of high-technology firms. *Courtesy of at Rensselaer*

Beginning in the early 1970s a significant number of architects and historians began to see Troy as a living museum of American commerce and industry in the nineteenth century. Still existing were evidences of the stores and factories which had made Troy a famous industrial center of the 1800s, as well as homes and public buildings designed by the nation's most prominent architects. Both the Hudson-Mohawk Industrial Gateway, formed in 1972 to preserve the industrial history of the area, and the Rensselaer County Historical Society have been active in preserving these architectural treasures and promoting Troy through tours, publications, and workshops related to this interesting heritage. In 1983 the Troy Liveability Campaign was founded to further promote the city as an exciting place to live. Bart Thibadeau of the Gateway is seen here guiding a tour of the Washington Park area in 1977. *G. Steven Draper photo; courtesy of the photographer*

191

During the past few years numerous Rensselaer County citizens have had the chance to serve as extras in the Hollywood films produced in this area. The Rensselaer County Court House served as a background for the period film *The Bostonians* in the early 1980s. More recently, Jack Nicholson and Meryl Streep were filmed at several locations in and around Troy during the production of *Ironweed*, a dramatization of the Pulitzer Prize winning novel of the same name, written by county resident William Kennedy. *J. S. Carras photo; courtesy of the* Times Record

Much of Troy's revitalization was made possible by its treasure trove of historically significant commercial structures. Troy boasts eight districts on the National Register of Historic Places. Development of the Quayside Apartments in the River Street Historic District shown here was made possible by a financing package which relied heavily on federal tax incentives for the rehabilitation of historic structures. The Downtown Troy Facade Revitalization Program, begun in 1977 by the Rensselaer County Historical Society and later administered by the City of Troy, was responsible for refurbishing dozens of building facades in the business district.

In addition to programs specifically oriented to historic properties, two agencies have been active in renovation for low and moderate income housing. Troy Rehabilitation and Improvement Program (TRIP), incorporated in 1968, is one of the most innovative low-income housing rehabilitation programs in the nation. Further aiding the revitalization of the city, Troy Architectural Program (TAP), founded in 1969, provides architectural design and planning services to low-income families, neighborhood groups and nonprofit organizations. The total impact of these programs won Troy the 1985 Main Street Award, presented annually by the Division of Economic Opportunity of the New York Department of State.

National Register Districts and facade improvement grant programs have had a similar impact on other towns in the county, refocusing resources on the existing building stock to preserve the county's rich heritage. *Michael McMahon photo; courtesy of the* Times Record

Troy's Facade Rehabilitation Program has restored many storefronts in the business districts of Troy and Lansingburgh. Pictured is a block of Second Avenue which underwent extensive work. *Gene Dzaman photo; courtesy of the* Times Record

RPI's late president, George M. Low, envisioned Rensselaer Technology Park on Route 4 in North Greenbush as an "ideal technological environment." This concept and its present reality are supported by the presence of major educational and research institutions, spurred by the business community, and aided by dependable financial assistance for qualified tenants, who find a pool of scientifically-trained professionals.

The tenants and their more than seven hundred employees represent a variety of disciplines. The Information Resources Company, a division of NYNEX (shown here) employs 350 people; there is a thirty-person consulting firm which is concerned with the latest developments in asbestos abatement, and the number of young, innovative research and engineering firms has continued to grow since the park first opened in early 1987. *Hughes Gemmill photo; courtesy of the photographer*

Troy began to regain the traditional appearance of a river port with the completion of the Riverside Park in 1982. The U.S. Coast Guard cutter *Raritan* took part in the dedication of the park which stretches from City Hall to the Troy/Green Island bridge. Opened in 1982, the park is an important part of the revitalization of Troy's waterfront. The new city hall, refurbished office and apartment buildings, new restaurants, and riverboats which offer sightseeing and dining have all helped to bring people back downtown.

Festivals in the park bring people from throughout the county to enjoy dancing, sample ethnic dishes, and listen to music. The Rensselaer County Council for the Arts has a very successful arts and crafts show here each June, and the Collar City Pops, started in 1984, performs here throughout the summer. *J. S. Carras photo; courtesy of the* Times Record

Fifty years ago C. W. Kelsey and George B. Cluett II formed the Rototiller Company, manufacturing cultivators for the home gardener. The company has evolved since then into Garden Way, Inc. In addition to manufacturing a variety of Troy-Bilt tillers, they promote effective home gardening with other products and literature.

The people of Rensselaer County come from all walks of life and all backgrounds. The county's story is the story of these people who live and work within its borders. Their strengths and resourcefulness have a local effect, shaping national trends and events into the history which is unique and particular to Rensselaer County.

The employees of Garden Way gathered here for the camera are only a fraction of the people of Rensselaer County, but the diversity within their group is a good image to carry with us as we move on into the county's next three hundred years of history. *Courtesy of Garden Way, Inc.*

Shown here is the Lansingburgh Fire Pumper
at Fire Company Headquarters, 115th Street
near First Avenue. *Courtesy of Frances D.*
Broderick

Bibliography

Anderson, George Baker, *Landmarks of Rensselaer County.* Syracuse: D. Mason & Company, 1897.

"The Approach." *Troy Record,* October 30, 1983.

"As In Days Gone By." Hoosick Falls, N.Y.: Hoosick Township Bicentennial Committee, 1976.

Beers. F. W. *County Atlas of Rensselaer, New York, From Recent and Actual Surveys and Records.* New York: F. W. Beers & Co., 1876.

Benjamin and Park, eds. *Cyclopaedia of Applied Mechanics.* New York: D. Appleton & Co., 1878.

Bennett, Ruth C. *The Grafton (N.Y.) Hills of Home.* New York: Vantage Press, 1974.

Bird. F. W. *The Hoosac Tunnel: Its Condition and Prospects.* Boston: Wright & Potter, 1865.

Broderick, Frances D. "The Manufacture of Brushes." *Northern Centinel,* June 14, 1977.

Broderick, Warren ., ed. *Brunswick. . .A Pictorial History.* Troy, N.Y.: Brunswick Historical Society, 1978.

Carpenter, Madolyn V. "Reviews and Reminiscences: A Brief History of the Town of Sand Lake." Sand Lake, N.Y.: 1979.

"Castleton-on-Hudson: A Village Walk." Tour Commission, 1977.

"The Challenge of Local History." Proceedings of Local History Enrichment Program, The State Education Department, Office of the State Historian, 1967-1968.

Craib, Stephanie H., and Roderick H. "Our Yesterdays, a History of Rensselaer County." Troy, N.Y., 1948.

Crandall, Patricia. "Melrose, Then and Now." Melrose, NY: Melrose Bicentennial Commission, 1976.

Dunn, Shirley. "Muitzeskill Hitoric District," The Historical Society of Esquatak, 1976.

"East Greenbush, N.Y." Souvenir program, East Greenbush Bicentennial Commission, 1976.

Ellis, D. M.; Frost, J. A.; Syrett, H. D.; and Carman, H. J. *A History of New York State.* Cornell: Cornell University Press, 1965.

Foerster, Bernd. *Architecture Worth Saving in Rensselaer County, New York.* Troy, N.Y.: Rensselaer Polytechnic Institute, 1965.

French, J. H. *Gazetteer of the State of New York.* Albany, 1860.

Funk, Robert. "Recent Contributions to Hudson

Valley Prehistory." *New York State Museum Memoir,* No. 22, 1976.

Gordon, Thomas F. *Gazetteer of the State of New York.* Philadelphia, 1836.

Gordon, William Reed. *Third Rails, Pantographs and Trolley Poles.* Privately published, 1973.

Harlow, Alvin F. *Steelways of New England.* New York: Creative Press, Inc., 1946.

Hayner, Rutherford. *Troy and Rensselaer County, New York: A History.* New York: Lewis Historical Publishing Co. Inc., 1925.

Hill, Florence M. *West of Perigo: Poestenkill Memories.* Troy, N.Y.: Whitehurst Printing, 1979.

Hill, Florence; Cuffe, Mary; and Sagendorf, Cathy, comps. & eds. *The Road Home: A Pictorial Hitsory of Poestenkill, New York.* Poestenkill, N.Y.: Poestenkill Bicentennial Commission, 1975.

Holloway, Joseph, ed. *As In Days Gone By.* Hoosick Falls, N.Y.: Hoosick Bicentennial Commission, 1975.

Huey, Paul R.; and Phillips, Ralph D. *The Early History of Nassau Village, 1609-1830.* Nassau, N.Y., 1976.

Jameson, J. Franklin, ed. "DeLaet's New World." *Narratives of New Netherland: 1609-1664.* 1909, reprint, New York: Barnes & Noble, Inc., 1967.

King, Eric. "History of Castleton." *Chatham Courier,* 1968.

Klopott, R. Beth. "The History of the Town of Schaghticoke 1676-1855." Doctoral dissertation, State University of New York at Albany, 1981.

Lansingburgh Historical Society, comp. *Lansingburgh, New York 1771-1971.* Lansingburgh, N.Y.: Whitehurst Printing, 1971.

Leary, Sister Mary Ancilla. *A History of Catholic Education in the Diocese of Albany.* Washington, DC: Catholic University of America Press, 1957.

Lohnes, Richard. "Schaghticoke Centennial Booklet 1867-1967." Schaghticoke, N.Y.: Schaghticoke Centennial Celebration Inc., 1967.

Lord, Philip L., Jr. *Mills on the Tsatsawassa.* Albany: State Education Department, Division of Historical and Anthropological Services, 1983.

Moore, H. Irving. *A Pictorial Reminiscence and Brief History of Lansingburgh, Rensselaer County, N.Y. Founded in 1771.* Troy, N.Y.: Privately Published, 1957.

Morison, Samuel E. *The Oxford History of the American People.* New York: Oxford University Press, 1965.

Nestle, David F. *A History of the Hudson Valley Railroad.* Privately Published, 1967.

Newton, Steven. "Walter A. Wood." *Working People,* vol. 2, No. 3, October/November 1986.

"1965 Survey of County Schools." Troy, N.Y.: League of Women Voters of Rensselaer County, 1965.

"Old Home Week—Hoosick Falls." Souvenir program, Hoosick Falls, N.Y.: 1911.

Olivo, Tracy. "A History of the Mary Warren Free Institute." unpublished paper, 1986.

Parker, Joseph A. *Looking Back: A History of Troy and Rensselaer County 1925-1980.* East Greenbush, N.Y.: Greenbush Historical Society, 1982.

Phelan, Thomas. *The Hudson Mohawk Gateway: An Illustrated History.* Northridge, Cal.: Windsor Publications, Inc., 1985.

Proudfit, Margaret Burden. *Henry Burden, His Life and a History of His Inventions Compiled from the Public Press.* Troy, N.Y.: Pafraets Press, 1904.

Rensselaer County 1791-1966 City of Troy 1816-1966. Troy, N.Y.: Rensselaer County Historical Society, Inc., Publications Committee, 1966.

"Resources and Attractions of Hoosick Falls, New York." Hoosick Falls, N.Y.: 1890.

Reynolds, Helen Wilkinson. *Dutch Houses in the Hudson Valley Before 1776.* 1929. Reprint. New York: Dover Publications, Inc., 1965.

Rezneck, Samuel. *Education for a Technological Society.* Troy, N.Y.: Rensselaer Polytechnic Institute, 1968.

Ringwald, Donald C. *Hudson River Day Line.* Berkeley, Cal.: Howell-North, 1965.

Ritchie, William A. *The Archeology of New York State.* Garden City, N.Y.: Natural History Press, 1969.

Rudolf, Frederick. "Emma Willard." *Notable American Women,* Vol. III, Cambridge, Mass.: Belknap Press of Harvard University Press, 1971.

Ruedemann, Rudolf. "Geology of the Catskill and Kaaterskill Quadrangle." *New York State Museum Bulletin,* December 1942.

"Schodack: Basis for Comprehensive Planning." Raymond, Parish & Pine, Inc., 1970.

Index

Shaughnessy, James. *Delaware and Hudson.* Berkeley, Cal.: Howell-North Books, 1967.

Shaughnessy, James. *The Rutland Road.* Berkeley, Cal.: Howell-North Books, 1964.

Stephentown Historical Album. Stephentown, N.Y.: Stephentown Historical Society, 1977.

Sylvester, Nathaniel B. *History of Rensselaer County, New York.* Philadelphia: Everts & Peck, 1880.

Upton, Charles W. "Eliza Kellas." *Notable American Women,* Vol. II, Cambridge, Mass.: Belknap Press of Harvard University Press, 1971.

Ure, Andrew, M.D. *A Dictionary of Arts, Manufactures and Mines.* New York: D. Appleton & Co., 1844.

Viens, Charles, and Young, Sanford. *Troy and New England Railway: 1895-1925.* Privately Published, 1976.

Vogel, Robert M., ed. *A Report of the Mohawk-Hudson Area Survey.* Washington, D.C.: Smithsonian Institution Press, 1973.

Waite, Diana S. *The Troy Gas Light Company Gasholder House.* Troy, N.Y.: Hudson-Mohawk Industrial Gateway, 1977.

Waite, John G., and Diana S., comp. *Industrial Archeology in Troy, Waterford, Cohoes, Green Island and Watervliet.* Troy, N.Y.: Hudson-Mohawk Industrial Gateway, 1973.

Walsh, Alice P. "Castleton: Whose Minding the Business?" *Chatham Courier,* 1982-1983.

Walsh, Alice P. "Schodack Central School: History of a Rural School District in the State of New York." Kinderhook, N.Y.: Stuyvesant Press, 1986.

Waterford to Whitehall. Waterford, N.Y.: Waterford Historical Museum & Cultural Center, Inc., 1968.

Weise, A. J. *City of Troy and its Vicinity.* Troy, N.Y.: E. Green, 1886.

Weise, A. J. *History of the City of Troy.* Troy, N.Y.: William H. Young, 1876.

Weise, A. J. *History of Lansingburgh, N.Y. from the year 1670 to 1877.* Troy, N.Y.: William H. Young, 1877.

Weise, A. J. *History of the Seventeen Towns of Rensselaer County.* 1880. Reprint. Troy, N.Y.: Rensselaer County American Revolution Bicentennial Commission, 1975.

Young, Sanford. *Village of West Sand Lake 1788-1790.* Privately published, 1977.

(Front row): Helen M. Upton, Eva Gemmill, Joseph A. Parker,
(Back row): Robert N. Andersen, G. Steven Draper, Rachel D.
Bliven, Hughes Gemmill.

About the Authors

Rensselaer County has a wealth of history which has been recorded over the years by many fine historical societies and local historians. Our author team was chosen to present as comprehensive a view of the county as possible. Each author dealt with a general subject area in which he or she was already well versed, researching and adding local facts to the general overview. Further coordination of the material was provided by the team captain.

Rachel D. Bliven, a graduate of Wellesley College and the University of Vermont, has degrees in Victorian studies and historic preservation. She is currently a free-lance writer and historical consultant for audio-visual productions. Among her recent projects has been an orientation film and exhibits for Troy's new Riverspark Visitor's Center in the Hudson-Mohawk Urban Cultural Park. As coordinator of the team, Ms. Bliven organized meetings, set the demanding timetable, then synthesized and edited all the information received. In addition she wrote the chapter introductions and researched and wrote the early history.

Robert N. Andersen, a native of Rensselaer County, is a Professor Emeritus of the School of Education, State University of New York at Albany. Much of his time is spent in volunteer work—teaching, writing, researching, and serving humanitarian projects. On the team Mr. Andersen dealt with the issues related to recreation and drew on his vast experience as a researcher for the Society to advise on many other subjects.

G. Steven Draper, an RPI alumnus, is a free-lance photographer who has researched and lectured widely on local rail history and architecture. He has been involved with the renovation of historic structures in Albany and Troy, including the Burden Iron Company Office building in Troy where he was resident caretaker for seven years. He currently serves on the boards of both the Hudson-Mohawk Industrial Gateway and Camp Chingachgook, the regional YMCA camp. Mr. Draper coordinated the information on transportation and was the team photographer, a critical and demanding chore in a pictorial history and one for which he is well qualified, both by his knowledge of local photographic collections and his technical expertise.

Eva Gemmill, a founding member of the Poestenkill Historical Society, has also been active in the Hudson-Mohawk Industrial Gateway. She has written about industrial history for the Gateway, and for the *Conservationist.*

Hughes Gemmill is a member of the Society for Industrial Archeology, and local and regional historical societies. As an engineer he has been involved in preservation of historic structures, and in research on old highways and turnpikes. The Gemmills bravely chose the areas of agriculture, commerce, and industry in the county, subjects both knew by virtue of their professional experience as well as their long-term interest in industrial history.

Joseph A. Parker joined the *Syracuse Post Standard* after graduating from Syracuse University. He started with The Record Newspapers in 1941 and served in the U.S. Army Signal Corps during World War II. At the end of the war he returned to the paper, holding a number of editorial positions as well as writing a local history column for fifteen years. He retired in 1981 and is the author of *Looking Back: A History of Troy and Rensselaer County 1925-1980.* As a long time local newspaper columnist and author, Mr. Parker was undoubtedly the most experienced writer. He was an astute observer of the political scene during the years which saw many governmental changes.

Helen Upton is a Professor Emerita of history at Russell Sage College, her alma mater. She is a trustee of the Shaker Museum, Old Chatham, the Shaker Heritage Society, Colonie, both in New York and Shaker Village in Canterbury, New Hampshire. She is also the author of *The Everett Report in Historical Perspective: The Indians of New York.* Mrs. Upton dealt with education in the county, an aspect of its history which has played a major role in the fame and economy of the area. Her research represents the most complete compilation on that subject accomplished to date.

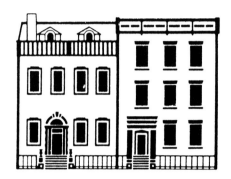

The Rensselaer County Historical Society is a private non-profit educational agency founded in 1927 by a group of thirty men and women from various parts of the county. Its chartered purposes are to collect, care for and make available to the public materials of all kinds related to the history of Rensselaer County and to promote that history in all its aspects. In 1952 the Society acquired through gift the Hart-Cluett Mansion, an 1827 Federal style townhouse on Second Street in the county seat of Troy, which it operates as an historic house museum. In 1982 it opened 57 Second Street next to the Mansion to house a gallery for changing exhibits, meeting room, museum shop and library of local history. Both buildings are on the National Register of Historic Places.

The Society's programs include lecture series, noon-hour programs, exhibits, school and adult tours, workshops, newsletters, fund-raising events, and historic preservation. It also sponsors the Associated Rensselaer County Historical Societies (ARCHS).

The Rensselaer County Historical Society is accredited by the American Association of Museums.